Health Care Will Not Reform Itself

A User's Guide to Refocusing and Reforming American Health Care

"Clear, concise, and compelling, George Halvorson's latest contribution clarifies why we must change, how we must change, what we must change, and when we must change. The answer is now. Drawing on the learnings from Kaiser Permanente's transformation to a fully digitally enabled, integrated system of care, George Halvorson shows all of healthcare how to focus on the right goals and improve our performance in reaching those goals. Let's get on with it!"

— Ian Morrison
Futurist; Author of "The Second Curve: Managing the Velocity of Change" and "Healthcare in the New Millennium"

"When running for office, President Obama pledged to expand health insurance coverage while reducing the cost of care by $2500 per year for the average family. Skeptics scoffed that industry insiders would block this goal in defense of their interests. Now George Halvorson, CEO of the nation's largest health care delivery system, says reducing costs while expanding coverage not only should be done, but can be done, and tells us how. His book highlights the important role and many forms of connectivity in health care: electronic medical records for patients and physicians, registries and care coordination programs for chronic illness, mandates and exchanges for health insurance, the alignment of culture and incentives among the many contributors to the wellbeing of patients."

— Dr. James Robinson, PhD, MPH
Professor of Health Economics, UC Berkeley

"George Halvorson offers a timely and compelling prescription to addressing the chronic ills of our health care system. One doesn't have to agree with every proposal to appreciate the extraordinary contribution he has made here. Students of health reform would do well to consider this book as an invaluable text for our national public policy debate."

— Tom Daschle, Former U.S. Senate Majority Leader

"George Halvorson's timing couldn't be better and his message couldn't be more valuable. He documents in clear, vivid prose why the health care system won't reform itself which all employers and payers need to understand so they don't miss this pivotal moment to dramatically reform health care. He offers information, evidence and practical solutions for aggressively attacking the "crushing burden of health care costs," as President Obama described our national challenge. Halvorson also provided ways we can sharply improve quality and safety, as well as save substantial dollars. He reminds us again, through many excellent examples, how essential it is to have electronic health records for effective, appropriate care at a reasonable cost. This book provides a great checklist for healthcare reform for the public and the private sector. I strongly recommend it."

— Helen Darling
President , National Business Group on Health

"Halvorson's simple, direct writing style is remarkable for its clarity. He takes complex problems and makes them understandable. Halvorson's experience as leader of one of the world's largest and most successful implementations of health information technology makes his insights into that subject particularly valuable."

— Dr. Alain C. Enthoven, PhD
Marriner S. Eccles Professor of Public and Private Management, Stanford University

Health Care Will Not Reform Itself

A User's Guide to Refocusing and Reforming American Health Care

GEORGE C. HALVORSON

CRC Press
Taylor & Francis Group
Boca Raton London New York

CRC Press is an imprint of the
Taylor & Francis Group, an **informa** business

A PRODUCTIVITY PRESS BOOK

Cover image: Nadav Kander/Gallery Stock

Productivity Press
Taylor & Francis Group
270 Madison Avenue
New York, NY 10016

Library of Congress Cataloging-in-Publication Data

Halvorson, George C.
    Health care will not reform itself : a user's guide to refocusing and reforming American health care / George C. Halvorson.
        p. ; cm.
    Includes bibliographical references and index.
    ISBN 978-1-4398-1614-1 (hbk. : alk. paper)
    1. Health care reform--United States. I. Title.
    [DNLM: 1. Health Care Reform--methods--United States. WA 540 AA1 H117h 2009]

RA395.A3H34495 2009
362.1'04250973--dc22   2009013219

Visit the Taylor & Francis Web site at
http://www.taylorandfrancis.com

and the Productivity Press Web site at
http://www.productivitypress.com

This book is dedicated to my son, Charles, who decided that we should take our vacation together this year to write stuff we both needed to write. This fourth book in my health care trilogy would not exist without him. His honors thesis seemed to go well, as well, so it was a good week for both of us.

Danke, Carlos.

Contents

Acknowledgments

I would also like to thank Christina Holmes, Victoria Meas, Mike Lassiter, Chris Stenrud, and Nate Dyke for their help in getting this book assembled, typed, fact checked, verified, and to the publisher on an incredibly tight time frame. Thank you all for a job well done.

Thank you to the caregivers at Kaiser Permanente, to the medical leadership team, to the KP operations and IT staff, and to the KP HealthConnect™ rollout team for giving me the real world examples that serve as proof points for the proposals and ideas that are embedded in this book.

Introduction

We have a really interesting, challenging, and extremely important problem to solve in America.

We need to bring down the cost of care.

And we need to improve the quality of care in the process.

Health care in America is badly organized, highly inconsistent, internally dysfunctional, sometimes brilliant, almost always compassionate, close to data free, amazingly unaccountable in key areas, too often wasteful, too often dangerous, and extremely expensive. Care costs more in America than it does anywhere else in the world — by every measure. Care costs more per person, more by the unit, more by the dose, more by the disease, and more in the aggregate. We spend far more than anyone else in the world on care, and we are alone among the industrialized countries in not covering all of our people. We need to do a lot better.

So what can we do about that issue? We actually can make care both better and less expensive. How can we do that? We need to reform the actual delivery of care.

We need to be very clear about what aspects of care we want to reform. We need goals — and then we need strategies to achieve those goals. Reforming care with no goals is almost always an exercise in futility, frustration, and/or irrelevance.

We need clear goals, a strategy to achieve each goal, and the tools necessary to achieve each strategy. Tools make huge sense when we have a strategy for their use. Tools generally make a lot less sense and add little value when we don't know either what we actually intend to do with the tool or what the tool is capable of doing.

Electronic medical records can be a wonderful tool if we know why we have them and use them well. And they can be a very expensive use of money if we just put them in place and then simply hope that something good will happen because they exist. The test of a good tool is whether it gets used — not whether it exists.

America definitely needs a clear care reform agenda. We have major performance shortfalls today. We get care wrong now for diabetics well over half the time. Kids with asthma get right care barely half the time. People who are depressed get right care less than a third of the time. Care in America definitely needs to be improved. Care improvement will only happen if we are absolutely clear on our goals — like cutting kidney failures in half — and then make the right changes in our care delivery systems, support infrastructure, and cash flow to make that goal a reality.

Half of the kidney failures in America should not happen. We will not cut the failures in half until we recognize exactly what steps we need to take to achieve that goal. Simply hoping that random and unconnected doctors and hospitals will serendipitously and spontaneously make a series of changes and somehow achieve at least semisystematic improvements in care delivery in 100,000 different places in any relevant time frame is pure magical thinking. The sheer logistical barriers to achieving serendipitous care improvements are insurmountable.

So we need focus. We need tools. And we also very definitely need to improve people's health.

FIX CARE — IMPROVE HEALTH

We need to fix care and we need to enhance health. We need half as many people to become diabetic and we need half as many diabetics to lose a limb or become blind. Those are both achievable agendas, but they are only achievable if we make the kinds of changes needed to affect care patterns, improve record keeping for care, create accountability for care, and positively influence the behavior of both patients and the people who deliver their care.

Better care usually costs less money. It costs a lot less to keep a congestive heart failure (CHF) patient out of the hospital than it does to help those patients return home from the hospital.

People with CHF are drowning in their own fluids. They are in pain, often in danger of dying, and generally have to breathe for periods of time through large and extremely uncomfortable tubes inserted down their throats. It's a horrible experience — and it should not happen at least half the time. We need to set goals to reduce those CHF crises by half — or more.

We now have a highly directional set of goals for the cost side of the problem. President Obama has called for us to reduce the premium costs needed to insure an average American family by $2,500 per family.[1] His stated belief is that it will be hard to cover everyone in America until we can bring down the costs of premiums paid by American families by about that amount.

Is that premium reduction possible? It can be — if we do a lot of things right. Opportunities exist to have a very direct impact on the specific premium costs President Obama is targeting. Look at the actual numbers.

The average total cost of care for a family in America right now is about $12,000 per family.[2] Reducing those costs by $2,500 means reducing them by roughly 21 percent.

What could we possibly do to reduce premium costs for American families by nearly 21 percent, and save roughly $2,500 per family in the cost of care?

UNIVERSAL COVERAGE IS A FIRST STEP

For starters, we need to cover everyone. That doesn't seem logical, but the truth is that covering everyone in the country can significantly reduce the price of insurance premiums needed to cover families in America.

Universal coverage, all by itself, could and should save us about half of that money. That is true because part of the money now charged to people in their private coverage insurance premiums really goes to offset the cost of providing unpaid care to uninsured people. If we can cover everyone in America, we can basically eliminate the very real cost shift to private insurance premiums that originates today from uninsured patients.

Where do premiums come from? Care costs. Medical costs and hospital costs basically create insurance premiums. So when American caregivers shift bad debt costs and increase their unit prices to insurers, the insurers automatically pass those cost increases along to everyone who buys insurance. That shifted amount now adds roughly $1,200 to the premium costs of each family contract.[3,4]

Universal coverage will solve that problem. If we cover everyone in America at adequate payment levels, that cost shift would not be needed. We could make it go away. We could save about $1,200 per family contract.

RECOVERING THE COST SHIFT BY REDUCING PRICE INCREASES

Recovering that money directly and immediately from caregivers' cash flows would, of course, probably be resisted to some degree by quite a few providers of care who might not want to reduce their current fees in any real way. The good news is we actually don't need to reduce current fees charged by these providers to recover the cost shift amount. We just need to slow a couple years of future fee increases. That can be done. We should be able to both document the actual current cost shift levels for providers of care and create a fair formula to reduce relevant provider fee increases for just a couple years to eliminate relative overcharges and "recover" the cost shift.

Provider prices usually go up by five percent or more per year,[5] so simply slowing many of those increases for a couple years for providers who have been shifting costs could give us the offsetting savings we need to meet half of President Obama's goal.

Students of health care costs and prices know that there is another significant cost shift that results from our Medicare and Medicaid programs paying many providers less than their full care costs for Medicare and Medicaid patients. The strategies outlined in this book do not touch that cost shift. It stays in place. That's an issue for another debate and another book. This approach only offsets the bad debt cost shift that exists today from fully uninsured patients.

WE NEED TO SPEND LESS ON CARE

But eliminating that cost shift from the uninsured patients obviously doesn't solve the entire $2,500 cost reduction goal set by President Obama. At best, it solves roughly half the target and it really doesn't bring down the total cost of care in America. It just brings down premium expenses. We also need to reduce actual care expenses. To achieve the other $1,300 in savings needed for family coverage, we will need to actually reduce the "run rate" cost of care. We will need to spend less money on care delivery.

Is that possible to do? Yes. Do we have to ration care or deny either services or care in some way to achieve those savings? No.

Rationing care is the wrong answer. We need to do the exact opposite. We need to reduce the costs of care by improving care. That strategy needs to be very clearly understood or it has no chance of success.

RIGHT CARE IS THE ANSWER

The answer is not to deny people needed care. The answer is to make very sure people in real need get the right care at the right time — and save money in the process.

"Right care" should be our goal. We need to hold ourselves as a nation to a higher standard of care delivery. We need patients in America to "get care right" a lot more often.

Again, the good news is that it is entirely possible to do. The opportunities and the money are there. The Commonwealth Fund did an extremely useful study slightly over a year ago to look at how much less money America could spend on care each year if we simply avoided "Potentially Avoidable Complications."

The researchers for the Commonwealth Fund looked at the actual insurance claims paid for five million people for two full years. The researchers used established science-based care guidelines to review all the claims paid for the five million people for selected categories of care expenses. Their goal was to find and measure care costs that would, could, and should have been prevented if the prior care and the current care for those individual patients had been better. The goal was to measure the potential cost benefit to America of getting care right.

The researchers focused their study primarily on a few key chronic conditions. That focus on a few conditions was a very smart thing to do because over 75 percent of care costs in America currently result from patients who have chronic conditions,[6,7] and 80 percent of those costs come from patients with both chronic care conditions and "co-morbidities."[8]

Co-morbidities means more than one disease. More than one disease means more than one doctor.

This book will deal in several places with the misfires, perverse consequences, and wasted resources that far too often result from unlinked and uncoordinated care when patients in America get care from multiple caregivers.

So how much money did the Commonwealth study say America could save by simply avoiding "avoidable care mistakes"? Half a trillion dollars.[9] Half a trillion dollars is a lot of money. It's more than enough money to achieve our goal.

SAVING HALF A TRILLION IS DEFINITELY ENOUGH

For the time period covered by the Commonwealth study, Americans were spending slightly over $2 trillion on our total health care. Saving half a trillion dollars in the context of a $2 trillion care economy by simply having fewer patients with unnecessary kidney failures, fewer avoidable amputations, reduced levels of heart by-pass surgery, and fewer crisis-level asthma attacks is both much better care and much less expensive care.

That amount of potentially saved money — for the years they studied — would have reduced the total cost of care in America by roughly 25 percent.

Those numbers do not include the equivalent amount of money we could save if we truly improve the health status of Americans. Those numbers are also huge but they will take years of hard work to achieve. These savings are the ones that just result from getting less care wrong.

Health care reformers need the courage to look at those "wrong care" numbers directly and decide whether it is economically viable to ignore that opportunity. Making changes in care delivery upsets political power bases, and will create some political backlash, but not making changes will doom us to unaffordable care. The sheer ethics of knowing that care can be better but isn't should drive us to make some politically difficult decisions.

The Commonwealth studies do not stand alone in telling us that those kinds of savings are possible. Millman actuaries have projected that an equivalent amount of money could be saved if the best practices of the best current care systems in America became the norm for American care delivery.[10] Dr. John Wennberg and the Dartmouth research have shown us that we can save an equivalent amount of money by simply bringing all caregivers in the country to the cost-effectiveness levels of the best performing regions of the country.[11]

Other studies have indicated that the potential savings from systematically improving care delivery could range as high as 30 to 40 percent.

But 25 percent is more than enough. Half of that amount is more than enough. Do the arithmetic. If we achieved even half of that potential "avoidable care" savings, that would be roughly a 12 percent cost reduction. Twelve percent of $12,000 is $1,440. If we add the $1,200 that can be saved by eliminating the current cost shift (because we will have covered everyone) to the new $1,440 that can be saved by getting care right, then the president's goal will be met. In fact, $2,640 in savings slightly exceeds the $2,500 goal.

AVOID AVOIDABLE MISTAKES

Those are all rough numbers, but they are real numbers. We have a lot of "avoidable" care expenses in this country. The potential savings are there. We may not hit each of those numbers exactly as we go forward to improve the costs of care, but we can come close enough to make the whole effort incredibly worthwhile. It's work that needs to be done. It's also work that can be done.

It verges on criminal that we alone of all industrialized countries do not have universal coverage. We should not have over 40 million uninsured Americans.[12] When we spend $2.5 trillion a year for care, everyone should be covered.

It's also true that when we spend $2.5 trillion for care — far more than anyone else in the world — we should get great care, not inconsistent, unaccountable, wasteful, sometimes dangerous and, far too often, structurally inconsiderate care.

Two and a half trillion dollars creates a cash flow that should be sufficient to both cover everyone in America and take care of everyone in this country really well.

My last book, *Health Care Reform Now!* (Jossey-Bass, San Francisco), outlined a plan to cover everyone in America. That book also talked about the disparities in care delivery and care outcomes that relate to poverty, race, and ethnicity. I stand by each of those positions today. This book is about making care more affordable by making it better.

That's what this book is all about. It's a call to action. It's a description of why health care in America is what it is and why it now costs what it costs. It's also a practical pathway to make care better. And more affordable.

We need to start with a solid knowledge base.

WE NEED THE RIGHT TOOLS

We won't achieve the goals we need to achieve in reforming American health care unless and until we understand exactly where we are now and until we collectively know exactly where we want to go.

We need to re-engineer key elements of care delivery and care financing. We need to introduce new care support tools — like care registries, electronic medical records, and a much higher level of connectivity.

"Connectors" can be almost magic when it comes to improving care. A major portion of this book is about the value of connectors. The original title of this book was "The Magic of Connectors."

We obviously need care that is connected — with caregivers appropriately connected to each other and to their patients. We need our database for health care connected so that it is patient focused rather than simply health care business unit and provider cash flow focused.

ALL OF THE INFORMATION ABOUT
ALL OF THE PATIENTS ALL OF THE TIME

We need to understand the role and value of connectors and linkages and we need to build them into our strategies for care. We ultimately need our physicians to have electronic access to "all of the information about all of their patients, all of the time." Until that happens, we need our physicians and other caregivers to have much better information about their patients and their care.

So this book is basically a kind of user's guide. It's not a theoretical or philosophical essay or a political advocacy piece. Hopefully, the topics raised and the suggestions made will be useful in helping inform the current debate about how to save $2,500 in the delivery of care and make care better in the process.

The final chapter of this book calls for a national commission on health care costs and quality. We don't need to reduce the per-capita costs of care in America. We do need to reduce the rate of increase in health care costs — and a sufficient decrease will make a huge difference in the health care budget and cost burden for America.

It will take quite a bit of political courage to get this job done. It will also take some targeted re-engineering of both care delivery and care financing. The alternative to courage and focused action is a continuation and probably a worsening of the status quo — and that is the outcome we really can't afford.

Enjoy the book. Be well.

1

Health Care Won't Reform Itself

We really do need to reform health care financing and delivery in America. We obviously can't afford to be on the path we are on now — headed for a cost level for health care that will make our industries uncompetitive in world markets and our government entitlement programs either insolvent, crippled, or so expensive that they will ultimately consume the entire federal budget and seriously impair most state budgets.

Something needs to be done. Before we can do what needs to be done, however, we all need to recognize one sad truth — health care in America will never reform itself.

Why would health care reform itself? The current health care infrastructure in the United States is generating nearly $2.5 trillion in revenue.[1] It is the fastest growing segment of the entire American economy. Nearly 17 percent of the total U.S. economy is now spent on health care expenses[2] and the revenue levels in health care are growing by 5 to 10 percent every year.[3]

People sometimes refer to health care as a failed, out-of-control portion of the American economy and wonder why health care doesn't do a better job of controlling costs.

We need to recognize the fact that if any other segment of the American economy were producing those kinds of revenue numbers, that industry would be considered a massive success. Imagine an automobile industry growing by 5 to 10 percent annually and expanding monthly as a percentage of our Gross Domestic Product (GDP). We would consider the car folks to be massive economic winners.

People who say health care is a "failed" segment of our economy are missing a very obvious point. We all need to look at the actual dollars being collected by the various businesses that constitute our health care infrastructure and recognize the fact that those businesses are absolutely not "failing" as an industry.

There is a lot of money in health care. Many thousands of health care businesses have set up shop in America. From a pure business perspective, those businesses are almost all economic successes — winners — not economic losers. Even in the current highly challenged economic environment, no one is suggesting that health care needs a bailout. Some health care entities are facing financial problems as the stock market is collapsing and fewer people have insurance. So some elements of health care are currently facing some economic challenges, but health care overall continues to be a huge and growing part of our economy, and is feeling less pressure than the rest of the economy even in bad times.

Why is that an important fact to understand and appreciate? That fact tells us that real health care reform will need to be externally triggered and imposed on the American health care economy.

Expecting our current massive, very well-financed, high-revenue, high-margin, high-growth, high-cost health care infrastructure to voluntarily take steps to reduce costs and prices, and expecting our care infrastructure to also voluntarily and spontaneously improve either care outcomes or care quality is unfortunately naïve. It is magical thinking to believe that health care delivery can, will, or even could reform itself in any significant way.

Think about the logistical issues involved. How would the current nonsystem reform itself even if it wanted to? What element or component of health care in America today could currently lead that reform?

Health care is the epitome of a nonsystem. Health care in America is comprised of hundreds of thousands of unrelated, unlinked, financially self-contained, self-focused, and self-optimizing business entities that are each set up to generate revenue and create financial success for themselves in the context and in the market model that is created by our current health care cash flow. Health care in America is a robust and growing nonsystem of immense size, scope, and scale. It is very well fed. By fees. Many fees. Fees are addictive. The infrastructure of health care in America is almost entirely funded by a steady and massive stream of fees and cash payments that have no linkage to either care quality, care efficiency, or care outcomes.

So why doesn't the huge current infrastructure of health care in America work consistently to either improve care or reduce cost? Why would it? "Good" care or "better" care does not increase market share or economic viability either for individual health care providers or for the total infrastructure of care. The actual quality of the health care product isn't measured, quantified, compared, or even identified in any useful way, and it is rarely a factor in making health care purchasing decisions.

So there is no economic reward for improving care. "Bad" care, however, can actually be very profitable for caregivers. A serious, painful, frightening, life-threatening asthma attack can easily generate $10,000 to $30,000 in hospital and physician charges and fees. Preventing that asthma attack earns no fee at all. We get exactly what we pay for. Many treat. Few prevent.

MANY TREAT — FEW PREVENT

There are now 18,000[4] billing codes in this country for separate units of care. Providers collect fees from insurers, government programs, and patients based on these billing codes. There are no billing codes for cures. There are also no billing codes for better outcomes, and there are no billing codes for care linkages.

So we have unlinked, inconsistent, often perversely incented, volume-generating caregivers — a vast unconnected and unmeasured array of care-based businesses who, in their entirety, collect nearly $2.5 trillion in revenue.

That massive amount of expense would not necessarily be a bad thing if we actually received full value for all the dollars that are spent. Health is a good thing to buy. Health care creates great jobs. Two and a half trillion dollars might actually be a very good price to pay for good health and great care.

STUDIES PROVE THE INCONSISTENCY OF CARE

Unfortunately, because "good" care is not a relevant factor in the American health care purchasing business model, care delivery in this country is inconsistent and almost idiosyncratic in its variations in patterns, care delivery, and use of resources. As a result, we do not get consistently high qualities of care for that $2.5 trillion dollars. Multiple studies have shown that sad reality to be true. We need to recognize that fact as well so we can try to figure out what can and should be done to make care better and more affordable in the United States. We need to recognize the fact that too much of the care delivered now is inconsistent, unfocused, uncoordinated, and even dangerous, and there are no financial penalties of any kind for that low level of performance.

John Wennberg and the very smart people at Dartmouth have repeatedly proven and documented the massive inconsistencies that exist from region to region in this country for both care outcomes and cost — with no positive relationships between better care and higher cost.[5]

This isn't new information. Dr. Wennberg has been sharing that data with America for a couple of decades. The value problem for American health care is actually getting worse instead of better. We now know many very sobering numbers about care inconsistency and excessive costs. Our health care policy community has chosen to quote the Wennberg data fairly often but uses it never.

Other studies show similar results about the quality and consistency of care. Rand did a wonderful study showing that barely half of adult Americans with significant diseases are currently receiving appropriate care for their conditions. That study looked at 20,000 patients over four years, and concluded that American patients received the "right" package of care roughly 55 percent of the time.[6] Fifty-five percent is a pathetically low number when we are spending $2.5 trillion to buy care.

More recently, a follow-up Rand study published in the *New England Journal of Medicine* showed that kids in America with serious chronic conditions like asthma are getting appropriate care barely 46 percent of the time.[7] That finding surprised a lot of people who believed we delivered more consistent care to children. Sadly, we now know that our kid care in America probably has even lower consistency levels than our adult care.

Asthma is the fastest growing childhood disease in America[8] and the new Rand study showed that 54 percent of the children diagnosed with asthma did not get recommended treatment.

CARE LINKAGE DEFICIENCIES ABOUND

Not only is care often falling short of some very basic standards, we also don't do a very good job of linking the care delivery needs of individual patients when each caregiver is a separate independent, self-optimizing, internally focused business entity and care function.

Multiple studies have shown that our caregivers do not link well with each other to coordinate care for too many patients. The Institute of Medicine did some excellent work on that issue in their report, "Crossing the Quality Chasm."[9] Everyone interested in health care reform in America should read that book.

NO MONEY, NO TOOLS, NO ACCOUNTABILITY FOR LINKAGES

So why don't caregivers in America link well with each other? The answers are painfully simple. Caregivers in this country don't usually link well because (1) they generally have no tools for linkages, (2) they receive no payment for linkages, and (3) no one is structurally held accountable for linkages for any given patient.

No tools, no money, and no one accountable is an obviously and inherently dysfunctional aggregation of care linkage impediments. The tool gap is a crippling issue all by itself. How can caregivers link with no linkage mechanisms? Caregivers in America almost always have no easy-to-use and ergonomically workable tools that they can use to connect care with other caregivers.

A recent Medicare study of care management approaches showed that the average Medicare patient in the study with co-morbidities had 17 separate doctors. Seventeen doctors — one patient.

Even caregivers who really want to coordinate care with the other caregivers who are treating the same patient almost always find themselves without the pure functional or logistical ability to consistently and easily link their care. There are almost no mechanisms for Dr. Jones to use to find out what Dr. Smith is doing for a patient they both share. Or for Dr. Jones to tell Dr. Smith what care he or she is providing to a mutual patient. Telephones exist, of course.

Each caregiver could, theoretically, stop seeing other patients for a few minutes and try to call each other up to talk about a given patient. That would, however, generally be a nonpaying, revenue-free diversion of valuable, highly billable time for the physician who does it, and even if American doctors tried to make those kinds of phone connections happen, there is no guarantee that the doctor they are calling would be available to have a conversation and share data. So those direct doctor-to-doctor contacts do sometimes happen — but not with any consistency or dependability. Some privacy laws can even make some of those contacts potential legal risks for the caregivers making or taking the calls. So linkages often don't happen.

The very nature of our piecemeal, splintered American care infrastructure causes many of those linkage problems.

Remember the core economic reality of American health care. Who delivers care? Care is delivered by a lot of independent business units. "Independent" is a key point to remember.

Almost without exception, each care business unit in America functions as a separate economic and operational entity. Pharmacies, hospitals, and physicians all tend to be totally separate cash-flows and completely separate information silos — usually not sharing data or patient-specific information with other caregivers or, very often, even with their own patients.

PAPER RECORDS ARE ENTIRELY AND ALMOST CRIMINALLY INADEQUATE

The lack of data sharing between caregivers is severely and fundamentally exacerbated by the fact that most medical information in America is now stored on paper medical records.

The paper records are an ancient data tool that is typically set up by each provider for each patient. That piece of paper and that data about a given patient are not usually shared in any way with other caregivers who treat that same patient. The paper records almost always sit in isolated filing cabinets in each provider's physical office area.

Paper is a bad mechanism for health care data storage. It's even worse for data linkages. Paper medical records are almost always incomplete. They tend to be functionally isolated, completely noninteractive, inherently inert, often inaccurate, sometimes illegible, and almost entirely useless for either tracking care across patients or populations or for coordinating care between caregivers.

It is almost criminal in this day of nearly complete and very sophisticated computer saturation and frequent interoperability for most other industries that data in health care is still almost entirely computer free.

The result of that lack of data is that even payers and patients who want to improve outcomes have a very hard time defining, measuring, tracking, or comparing outcomes, and there is no good way for patients to have anyone track or oversee the process, outcomes, and quality of their own care.

PROVIDERS DON'T CREATE THE ECONOMIC REALITY

We can't blame providers of care for the financial incentives that make up their economic reality. Many providers of care in America would actually prefer a different economic model and a different reward system. Many care providers know all too well that separate and unlinked fees paid for 18,000 separate units of care often are not the best way to buy or sell care. But providers don't create their own economic environment. They live, function, and do business in the economic context that this country has created for American care delivery and financing.

And, the truth is, providers do live well enough in this environment to generate a total billing stream that acquires roughly $2.5 trillion in cash each year from patients and other payers in America.

IS CARE TOO COMPLEX TO COORDINATE ANYWAY?

Some people believe that care delivery is inherently so complex and so piecework focused that caregivers could not and would not be able to re-engineer care even if the financial model of American health care somehow encouraged re-engineering.

That is not true. There are huge and somewhat obvious opportunities to influence the health care spending level in America while either holding quality levels steady or improving them by simply re-engineering key elements of care delivery. Re-engineering works in health care just like it does in every other major industry.

The Virginia Mason Clinic in Seattle did a great project a couple of years ago re-engineering one of the key rapidly expanding functions of modern health care.[10] They — as a world renowned multispecialty group practice — looked at their imaging functionality — their total set of x-rays, ultrasound, CT scans, and MRIs used for particular patients. The specialists at the clinic worked as a team to identify best practice care protocols for their imaging process. They relied on medical science and on their professional judgment as medical experts. Their goal as medical professionals was to make sure all patients got the exact imaging each patient needed.

They succeeded. They put "best practice" protocols in place and used them for every patient who needed imaging. By doing the right thing for every patient, Virginia Mason improved care.

They also reduced the total number of images they did for those patients by about 30 percent. The cost of care went down. When the clinic doctors put solid science-based selection and referral criteria in place, the number of images done by the clinic literally decreased. It was actually much less expensive to get care right.

The problem, of course, is that the Virginia Mason Clinic is an economic entity. A self-sustaining economic entity. The clinic is — in the real world — a business as well as a giver and provider of care.

So how did making care better affect the clinic financially? Payers had paid very nice fees to the clinic for each of those scans in the past.

The clinic budget and business model had long relied on the revenue flow from those volumes of fees that had been generated for years by doing multiple levels of imaging in the old patterns. The new approach significantly cut the number of scans. That cut the number of fees. That, of course, reduced the flow of cash to the clinic. Their radiology department, in particular, took a loss of revenue from those new higher quality care protocols. The result of "doing good" was not to "do well." Jobs were threatened. Margins disappeared. Folks were very unhappy. So the real world reward to the clinic for getting care right was to lose money.

Think about that very real economic situation. Why would any care system that exists today as a business entity in the American health care economy decide to voluntarily go down that type of best practice "care improvement" pathway when the end point of the process was both to lose money and weaken themselves financially?

People who can get through medical school tend to be very smart people — too smart to ruin their own businesses and cash flow by becoming more efficient, generating less volume, and potentially going insolvent in the process.

That potential loss of revenue from improving care is a harsh reality that American economists and policy gurus need to understand if we really want to reform care delivery in this country. A few large care systems in America — like The Geisinger System, The Mayo Clinics, Virginia Mason, Intermountain Healthcare, Health Partners, Group Health Cooperative of Seattle, and the Kaiser Permanente caregivers — are doing important work that shows how care can be improved with systematic process re-engineering. Those efforts are works of ethical commitment, not economic self-interest, and the caregivers involved typically end up with fewer billable events, less revenue, and no economic reward for their efforts. In fact, economic penalties are the usual outcome for most care systems.

IN OTHER INDUSTRIES, LOWER PRICES INCREASE SALES

In almost all other industries, increased efficiencies result in better prices and better prices result in either higher unit profits or more sales.

In health care, however, total sales usually don't go up when some level of care delivery efficiency happens. "Sales" actually go down when unnecessary scans aren't done, or when unnecessary asthma attacks or heart attacks or strokes don't happen. Better care often means that caregivers sell fewer "pieces" of care. So why would caregivers who understand that reality and who want to maintain their cash flow re-engineer care? Don't blame caregivers. No other industry would increase their own internal levels of efficiency either if the result of successfully re-engineering their product's production process was fewer sales, lower revenue, less cash, and vanishing profits. Easy unit-of-care sales that would have simply been there as in-the-pocket revenue for the health care company or business unit can very easily simply disappear anytime providers do real and effective care improvement re-engineering.

Think like an economist. Remember how the business model for care works. Health care doesn't sell a total package of services for a package price. Health care sells units of care by the piece. Efficiency in care delivery very often directly reduces the number of care pieces that are sold.

So in the current economic model of selling care by the piece, this involves caregivers not benefiting in any immediate way by bringing down the total or package price of care. Based on that model, it is pretty clear that most care teams and independent care delivery business entities will not spend a lot of voluntary effort to reduce unit prices or improve the total efficiency of care delivery. We will not achieve the president's goal of reducing family premiums by $2,500 per family if we wait for caregivers to voluntarily become more efficient and reduce the ongoing cost of their care.

SCREW-UPS CAN BE PROFITABLE

That's actually not, however, either the most fascinating or the most frustrating aspect of the current set of financial incentives we have created for the care business infrastructure of this country. The really frustrating and painful reality is that American caregivers often make more money when care gets screwed up. Bad care can be very profitable care. Inadequate care improves cash flow. Mistakes can increase revenue. How can that be?

One of the great simultaneous ironies and tragedies of American health care is that some of the most expensive and high-revenue patients for the total care infrastructure are actually patients who were personally damaged by the care system. People being treated in hospitals who end up with bloodstream infections, for example, or people who suffer from hospital-induced pneumonia generally create huge revenue flows for both hospitals and doctors.

A simple $20,000 surgery patient who ends up with a serious bloodstream infection after having surgery can turn the $20,000 expense into a very profitable $100,000 hospital bill. Some caregivers say that large bill is entirely appropriate, because they need to provide a lot of care to a patient with a bloodstream infection and, in the real world, those infections "just happen."

The truth is, however, in most cases, those kinds of postsurgery infections can be almost entirely prevented if hospitals do their jobs really well. Some really well-managed hospitals have recently managed to go for years without one single infection. But preventing all of those infections is hard work. It takes consistent, patient-focused vigor and rigor on each level of infection risk. It isn't easy — but it can be done.

Hospitals in America, however, don't get paid more money if they do great work and are completely infection free. They do get paid a lot more money for patients with infections.

So the irony is that a $100,000 horrible care experience for that patient that creates pain, injury, fear, significant damage, and sometimes death can be one of the most profitable things that a hospital can do. Those infections are included in the kind of "avoidable care" events that the Commonwealth study, cited in the introduction to this book, believed could allow Americans to save half a trillion dollars by "getting care right."

Our current payment system has elements so perverse that completely preventing misery and avoiding all bloodstream infections is simply and completely unrewarded, but creating great pain and misery and suffering can be richly rewarded.

SCREW-UPS AREN'T DELIBERATE

No hospital anywhere in America would ever subject a patient to that horrible level of pain, misery, and risk of death to generate revenue. That absolutely isn't the point. The point is that we don't do enough to prevent those situations from happening — and caregivers almost always make money when they do. We should use our cash flow mechanisms very strategically and deliberately to reduce those risks — and we should not reward care delivery failures that could have been prevented by the caregivers. Medicare is beginning to take a leadership role in this area of care financing — refusing to pay for a series of "never" events.

This book will address "never" events later. "Never" events are true screw-ups (like wrong site surgery) that should almost never happen. Those events should be extremely rare. When they do happen, they definitely should "never" be paid for or rewarded.

WE NEED THE COURAGE TO REFORM CARE

So what needs to be done about American health care? We need to reform care delivery. We need better care, better outcomes, better data, better informed provider choices, better care option choices, and higher levels of accountability for care improvement and care results. We need the courage to actually reform care and the operational insight to know functionally how that can be done.

Better care could actually save us a lot of money as a nation. In fact, the sad and challenging truth is that we can't really bring down the rate of increase in the cost of care until we commit to actually improving care.

WE NEED UNIVERSAL COVERAGE

We also need everyone in this country to have health care coverage. Care reform and coverage reform should be a tightly wrapped and closely interwoven package. We need to tie care improvement very closely to universal coverage as an integral part of the total reform package.

Frankly, we need to cover everyone, so that we can improve care for everyone. Why do we need everyone to have health care coverage? One very practical reason is that we very much need everyone in America to be in the health care database for both care improvement and care accountability. We can't improve care for heart patients or asthmatics or diabetics until we can both track that care for all diabetics, and asthmatics, and heart patients, and get needed information to caregivers to help link care for individual patients. Care could be a lot better if it were more consistent and better connected.

The introduction to this book mentioned the Commonwealth Fund study that looked at how much money could be saved in this country if we simply got care "right." It was a very useful study. The researchers who did the study looked at a claims payment database of roughly 5,000,000 people.

They looked at how much care cost when care was done well and how much more health care cost when there were obvious "avoidable" events — like infections or badly managed and avoidable complications.

The researchers concluded that the potential savings from American physicians and hospitals simply avoiding "avoidable care complications" was over half a trillion dollars. If the total revenue stream for care is now $2.5 trillion and we can save half a trillion dollars by getting care right, that would seem to argue that our health care reform energies should be focused in that direction. The Milliman studies and the Wennberg data sets point us in exactly the same direction.

So what can we do? And what should we do next? The next chapter of this book deals with the real cost drivers for American health care. That chapter outlines where we are spending our health care dollars now and why care expenses are increasing.

TOOLS NEED A USE OR THEY ARE USELESS

Other chapters in this book explain several of the specific tools we need to put in place to functionally improve care. Those tools include operating systems, computer systems, data, care protocols, and changes in our health care benefit structure and cash flow.

Tools make little or no sense if we don't know what we are trying to do. A hammer can be a great tool, but if our current need is to cut wood rather than pound something into wood, even a truly lovely hammer is the wrong tool for right now. A number of health care policy thinkers have spent quite a bit of time recently talking about and advocating a number of specific tools that might be lovely tools, but aren't what we need to do right now.

Tools need to result from a strategy. We need to start with a clear agreement on what we really need to do to improve care. We need a real level of focus about our agenda and then we need the right tools to achieve our agenda.

We need to know collectively exactly which elements of care we should focus on improving first and which care support tools are needed to help us achieve that specific level of targeted improvement. Electronic support tools become very obviously useful when we start thinking about the real world steps we need to take to significantly improve care.

We also need to look at financial tools. Incentives do work magic in health care. We need to know how we can tweak or restructure the payment approaches that are used for key and targeted elements of care so that we can change the delivery of care to a more focused, process-based mode. Behaviors follow cash flow, so we need to look at those places where we can decide to modify the cash flow of health care to get caregiver behaviors and patient behaviors to change.

STRATEGIC MODIFICATIONS ARE NEEDED

We need to recognize the reality unintentionally imposed on us all by the current massive, well-financed, financially comfortable infrastructure of economically suboptimizing independent caregivers. We need to be very honest with ourselves. The current fee-for-service–based infrastructure of a great many independent, unlinked, unconnected, economically self-focused business entities delivering and selling units of care actually can't be modified very much or very quickly.

Keep in mind that 10 percent of our patients incur almost 80 percent of our total care costs. Five percent incur about half of the total costs of care. We can have a huge impact on care costs and care quality by making care better coordinated for about five percent of our total patient population. That is entirely doable if we choose to do it.

We can't force independent American caregivers to merge involuntarily into teams — and we can't force separate caregiver business units into true and complete economic consolidations. But we can use both cash incentives and cash flow to persuade independent providers to function cooperatively as "virtual teams" for the care of an extremely important, high-cost, and high-need targeted population of patients. That work of creating "virtual" connectivity can be done without forcing hostile or unwilling provider mergers. Ideas about how to achieve "virtual" mergers in important areas of care are described later in the book.

Because the fruits of the current nonsystem are largely a consequence of the cash incentives that exist today, we need to selectively modify some of those incentives to achieve many of our care goals.

The current nonsystem of health care will never voluntarily reform itself. It will not spontaneously become more efficient or more effective. It is what it is — with a vast current inconsistency in performance that ranges from great care to dangerous care — and it will take a clear plan and strategy to seriously improve that level of performance.

We need to identify a few areas of targeted behavior — like coordinating care for individual patients — and we need to modify the cash flow for care to either incent or require those behaviors to happen. We can't change everything in American health care, but we can change some important things, and those changes can make a big difference in the quality and cost of our care.

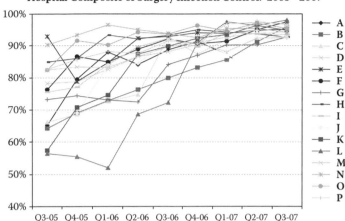

Figure 1.1   Hospital Safety Results

The hospitals shown in Figure 1.1 took a collective, systematic approach to care improvement. They started with goals, figured out processes, implemented new approaches and practices, and lives were saved. Fewer patients went through the hell and pain of postsurgery infections.

That improvement did not happen because a bunch of independent doctors and hospitals coincidently and separately changed their approach to care. It was a systematic change based on goal setting and process reengineering.

These hospitals significantly reduced the numbers of infections in three years to the point where the best hospital in year 1 did not do as well as the worst hospital in year 3. That is wonderful for the patients who did not have an infection. Perversely, in the fee-for-service world, the old high levels of infections would have generated many millions of dollars in additional revenue pay for those hospitals. That financial penalty for doing good work in care delivery needs to be understood. And — to get all hospitals in America on this path — we need to stop rewarding those kinds of infections.

This book is written from a fairly practical perspective. It isn't basically academic or theoretical or even political. It's functional. It's basically intended to be an operations guide for several aspects of care improvement.

Before looking at how we can change the delivery of care, let's take a look at some of the specific issues and forces that are driving care costs in America up today. That's the next chapter of this book.

2

Why Are Health Care Costs Going Up?

There is a huge amount of confusion in this country about why health care costs and health care premiums are going up. Most conversations on that topic sound a lot like the old "blind men and the elephant" fable — where the blind man who has hold of the tail thinks the elephant is a snake and the blind man touching the shoulder of the beast thinks the elephant is a wall. Just about everyone interested in health care reform has his own pet culprit as the key and primary cost driver for care. Drug costs, drug company profits, imaging costs, physician fees, hospital costs and hospital cost shifts, billing fraud, insurance company overhead, administrative overhead, malpractice suits, defensive medicine, primary care shortages, regulatory paperwork, and medical technology expansion all have their advocates as being the key cause of health care cost increases. Those factors all play a role in health care cost increases — and none of them, by themselves, explains very much of the cost situation.

So very few current debates on care costs deal with any real issues that are sufficient in themselves to truly impact the cost of care. And almost none of those conversations have the ability to answer one of the most frequently asked questions about care costs: "Why are health care costs in this country going up faster than the general rate of inflation?"

That's a really good question. It needs to be answered. If we can't answer that question, then we will obviously have a very difficult time ever actually bringing health care cost increases down to anything close to the general rate of cost inflation for the rest of the economy.

So what is the answer to that question? Why are health care costs going up more rapidly than the rest of the economy? What does the whole health care cost elephant look like? Let's look at the key cost drivers for care.

NORMAL INFLATION IS THE BOTTOM LINE, FIRST LEVEL, AND BASIC COST DRIVER FOR HEALTH CARE COST INFLATION

The truth is, health care cost increases in America basically actually start with simple inflation — standard, everyday, very basic, run of the mill, completely normal cost inflation. The first level cost driver every year for health care is identical to the foundational cost driver for all other American industries — pure, ongoing, and routine inflation of the basic costs of doing business in this country.

Salaries in health care settings go up every year, just like they do in every other segment of the economy. Heating and energy prices go up every year. The costs of construction, postage, transportation, essential goods and services, and facility maintenance go up every year for everyone. At a very basic level, all of the hundreds of thousands of independent businesses who deliver health care face the same set of inflation factors as every other business in America. They use the same electricity and buy the same paper clips and copy machine paper as every other business in America.

So when we ask why health care costs go up faster than normal inflation, we need to start with the logical and — when you think about it — fairly obvious fact that cost increases in health care start with the same basic inflation rates as every other area of the economy. Basic inflation is line 1 on the cost-driver chart.

WORKER SHORTAGES ADD TO COST INCREASES FOR CARE

Then we need to add on a set of costs that are unique to health care. For starters, there aren't enough trained health care workers in this country. Health care is facing serious worker shortages in quite a few categories of the work force. Many other industries have a surplus of available workers. Health care does not. Health care currently hires its work force from a shrinking and increasingly inadequate pool of skilled health care workers.[1]

Why is that relevant to annual health care cost increases? Workplace shortages naturally increase the cost of labor in health care at a slightly higher rate — because any economist can tell you that worker shortages in any industry tend to create additional wage inflation in that industry for those specific categories of workers.

So annual wage and salary increase rates for a large proportion of the actual jobs in the health care work force currently tend to be a bit higher than average wage inflation levels for jobs in most other American industries.

What are the most relevant health care work shortages? Many articles and studies have been done that describe the worker shortage in some detail.

We have a significant nursing shortage in many areas of the country. Pay for nurses on the West Coast of the United States has had an inflation level higher than other jobs in that same geographic area for the last several years.

We also have shortages of lab techs, radiation techs, medical assistants, medical radiographers, medical transcriptionists, pharmacists, pharmacy assistants, physical therapists, dentists, dental hygienists, and dozens of other health care support positions that require various levels of specialized training.[2]

Current vacancy rates in a wide range of health care job classifications range from 5 percent to 18 percent — and those deficits are expected to increase significantly over the next five years.[3]

Some of the biggest current future worker shortfalls are in a couple of medical specialties.

We are on the verge of a huge shortage of primary care physicians. We need primary care doctors to do the basic and fundamental work of making sure patients receive optimal care. Most other western countries have over half their physician work force in primary care.[4]

In the United States, we now have less than 40 percent of our doctors in primary care practices[5] — and the really alarming information we need to recognize is that only two percent of the medical students in America who picked medical school residencies in 2008 selected primary care as their specialty of choice.[6]

The number of geriatricians is also shrinking, going from 9,000 in the country a decade ago to less than 7,000 today.[7] Our population is getting older, and the number of geriatricians is shrinking. That is not a good thing.

Overall, 98 percent of our medical students now choose nonprimary care specialties.[8] Other Western countries deliberately ration the number of medical school openings that exist for specialty and subspecialty care. Why do they ration those openings? Because these countries want to keep their local primary care physician percentages high. This country has never successfully rationed anything in health care from a strategic policy viewpoint — so that strategy of rationing medical residencies is highly unlikely to be useful here.

Think like an economist. Why are doctors in training here not selecting primary care as their career path of choice? Cash. Money is a major factor. Most new subspecialists make roughly twice as much money as most new primary care doctors.[9] Over a career, subspecialists can make three to four times as much money as primary care doctors.[10] When new doctors come out of medical school deeply in debt and then make a personal decision to practice in primary care, their personal debt burden can extend for decades. Debt repayment can take a big chunk out of every primary care doctor's paycheck for a very long time.

Subspecialists can usually pay the same level of debts off much more quickly and also have a lot more money from each paycheck for their personal use while the debts are being repaid.[11]

When you compare physician income levels in the United States with European countries, we pay about the same for our primary care doctors — and we pay roughly 2.6 times more than Europe for our specialists. (See Figure 2.1.)

Why is that fact relevant to the cost increases we are seeing and will see for American health care? Costs will go up for our shrinking pool of primary care doctors faster than normal inflation. We will obviously need to pay primary care doctors better in the future.

The debt burden is only part of the problem. We also don't reward primary caregivers very well for patient care. Highly imbalanced payment levels by our Medicare programs for primary care procedures and specialty procedures are a major cause of the movement away from primary

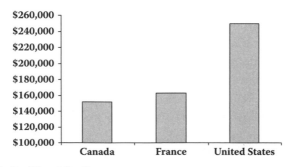

Figure 2.1   Medical Specialist Income

care as well. Medicare pays very low fees for primary care services and much higher fees for specialty care services.

So we can expect to see a bidding war in the private market for primary care doctors over the next several years. That will increase the rate of costs for health care well beyond inflation for those caregivers.

As we figure out how to get more doctors into primary care, we will also need to look at how to incent more physicians to be general surgeons, emergency room physicians, and geriatricians. We are already very much medically underserved in many American emergency rooms — and as noted earlier, our geriatrician shortage is already shocking, particularly in the face of a rapidly aging population.

So when we are calculating the reasons why health care costs are going up faster than inflation, we need to add in both the costs of present and of future health care worker shortages.

We also need to remember that the starting place for quite a few health care income levels in the United States is significantly higher then the monies paid to comparable categories of health care workers in Canada or most of Europe. Surgeons in the United States often start at a pay scale 40 to 50 percent higher than the amounts paid to those same categories of surgeons in Toronto or Paris.[12] But that's another whole set of relative cost issues that are outside the scope of this book.

NEW TECHNOLOGY, NEW TREATMENTS, AND NEW DRUGS INCREASE COSTS

That's just the start. Then, on top of the additional costs that result from health care worker shortages, we need to add on another whole set of costs that are basically unique to health care.

The third major cost driver for health care deals with new technology, new treatments, new procedures, and new pharmaceuticals that are introduced regularly into the American health care economy and care infrastructure. *New* is the key word. Health care is full of new developments. New scanners, new devices, new treatments, and new pharmaceuticals are introduced every month into American health care. Go to any medical convention, hospital convention, and/or biotech convention and simply visit the exhibit hall to get a glimpse of the kind of "new" things that are being introduced to care. Check out the "Clinical Technology Reference Guide," produced annually by the Health Care Advisory Board, to get a sense of new developments in the pipeline. The pipeline is full. New developments are developing daily. These new developments and new approaches create both new care results and new care costs. Those "new care" costs are being introduced every year in addition to — and on top of — the normal inflation rates for current and existing patterns of treatment and approaches to care. When new treatments, devices, or pharmaceuticals replace old drugs or devices, the new version typically both does more and costs a lot more.

This is not a minor cost item. The Congressional Budget Office (CBO) recently estimated that at least 40 percent of care cost increases over the past decade have arisen from new approaches to care and new delivery tools.[13] New implants, transplants, procedures, prosthetics, and diagnostic tools emerge constantly — and they all add regularly both to the functional capability of the care system and the direct cost of care. (See Figure 2.2.)

It's very easy to understand why new drugs and new care techniques are emerging. People want better care. Care, we all know, has yet to achieve perfection. Not everyone is cured, saved, sufficiently enhanced, or fully repaired by current levels of care. There are lots of opportunities for improvement in many areas of care. Those improvements happen regularly in the American health care economy because the business model for funding technological improvements is extremely cash rich in this country. There is currently a huge and very profitable market in America

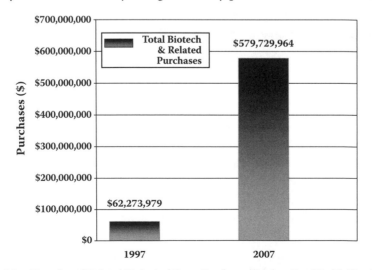

Figure 2.2 Biotech and Related Biological Drug Purchases Total — One Health Plan Total

for many categories of new and improved care-related equipment, services, treatment devices, drugs, tests, and care delivery techniques.

New treatments emerge constantly, and they are used when they become available, particularly if they generate more revenue for either hospitals or for the physicians who use each of the new approaches.

The use of new imaging and testing technology grows at an even faster rate when the caregivers themselves own the imaging or testing equipment and get to charge patients for the use of the machinery.

FEW STANDARDS OF VALUE EXIST

There are very few standards applied in the United States relative to the comparative value or usefulness of each new device or approach. Any attempt to add evaluation processes into the current American economic model of health care technology or procedures is usually fiercely resisted by both the health care business units involved and by the American consumer. Medicare failed miserably recently when it tried to require that the CT scans that are increasingly being used to find and diagnose non-symptomatic heart disease should be substantiated and validated by some level of scientific evidence about the relative value of the scans.[14]

Medicare lost that battle hands down. Why did Medicare attempt to slow down the use of those scans? The people at Medicare noticed that one of their fastest growing cost categories was CT scans that were being done simply to proactively "prospect" for possible heart damage or risk factors for basically nonsymptomatic Medicare patients. More than $14 billion worth of those screens were done in just one year and the number of scans being done was growing rapidly.[15]

The Medicare leadership pointed out that there was no solid science showing any significant medical benefit from those purely "exploratory" scans.

Ideally, doing a noninvasive scan that can be as accurate or more accurate than a truly physically invasive procedure is a good thing. In some cases, avoiding a physical probe or mechanical insertion and replacing it with a scan is a major improvement in patient care. It's also true that the science of scanning is constantly improving, and the likelihood is high that scans will, at some point, replace even more instances of invasive cutting, probing, and testing.

That isn't the point of this example. The point is that for the heart scans being done, there was no in-place body of evidence showing that they added value. There was, however, a set of caregivers who profited significantly by doing those scans.

What was the result? The large number of American heart doctors who own their own CT machines and who now earn up to 60 percent of their personal revenue doing those particular scans[16] played their own political cards with members of the U.S. Congress extremely well. In the end, Medicare simply surrendered, saying, very honestly, that these scans aren't the only thing Medicare pays for that isn't scientifically validated. Medicare was simply outgunned. Many patients wanted those scans. Very successful ad campaigns have promoted the use of those scans.

So the simple lack of science about the value of the scans didn't slow down the growth rate for the product or growth in the number of patients who were scanned.

Medicare is trying now to avoid paying for similar scans as an alternative to colonoscopies — hoping to wait until the technique proves itself before opening the door to millions of colon scans. The jury is still out on whether Medicare will be able to hold that particular line.

OTHER COUNTRIES USE SCREENING PROGRAMS FOR "NEW" CARE

That is, fairly often, the American way of health. Profitable care happens. We do so many CT scans in this country that some experts believe that 1.5 percent to 2 percent of all new cancers may already be attributable to radiation from those scans.[17]

New stuff is often very good stuff. Everyone wants the best new scan, the best new painkiller, and the best new artificial knee. Everyone wants the new biogenetic drug that extends life for cancer patients or other dire-disease patients by another month, another week, another day, or another year.

In most other countries, those categories of high-tech, high-cost treatment changes go through some kind of a screening or evaluation process. The British government uses NICE — the National Institute for Clinical Excellence — to measure the cost/benefit ratio of new approaches. Any proposed treatment changes, drugs, or pieces of technology that flunk the objective, data-rich NICE screen do not get introduced into the National Health Service. There has been absolutely no comparable scientific or value-based screen in the United States. Most private payers and governmental agencies in America pay for most new care and new technology almost all of the time. There have been very few exceptions. The new "Recovery" package has embedded in it a plan to begin to do a slightly more organized level of technology and process assessment in the United States. That approach is long overdue. But we don't know yet how well the new process will function when the political forces and "special interests" have finished influencing the actual role and operations of the new agency. When major drug companies spend $29 billion a year just on advertising to increase sales,[18] they are not very likely to want any process functioning that will evaluate how well their products actually work. Expect major resistance to that whole evaluation effort — probably disguised as consumer protection of some kind.

UNTESTED, PURELY EXPERIMENTAL, UNPROVEN CARE

The truth is, of course, up until now, just about everything that works to any degree has been covered in the United States.

Some levels of purely experimental, untested, and completely unproven care have initially not been covered by either governmental or private payers in this country, but even those entirely experimental procedures tend to become a covered benefit in America as soon as they are proven to work at even the most modest performance level.

THE DILEMMA — FOR SOME PATIENTS, THERE IS NO OTHER HOPE

The question of whether unproven, untested, highly experimental procedures should be covered is a serious, sometimes painful, and often challenging policy and ethical dilemma because it often is true that no standard care approaches that are available to the caregivers will work for some dire-need patients. Many of the patients in those fairly rare but sometimes highly visible situations do have a high probability of death with little hope that any "proven" treatment will work. Paying for experimental care directly creates a form of "experimental treatment" tax for payers. When an experimental procedure is covered, the new cost is simply spread across all people who pay premiums or pay taxes depending on who the payer is.

CAREGIVERS SOMETIMES OWN THE BUSINESSES

From the perspective of economic incentives, it often seems a little strange that the media covering those cases almost never notice when the caregivers who are proposing to do the procedure are sometimes personally receiving a lot of money to do the "experiment."

Both the pure ethical high ground and the financial motivation assessment in those cases are sometimes eroded a wee bit by caregivers who say, "I won't save this patient until someone pays me to do it. I will let them die unless you pay me." Then, when they have drawn their own clearly finance-based personal line in the sand, they sometimes publicly say that the payer who doesn't choose to write the check to them, for "experimental" care is actually the party in the situation who is "making an economic decision" about the life of a patient.

Interesting thought process. In many cases, of course, the recommended procedure involves teams of people and the whole funding stream is a lot more complicated than that. But sometimes it isn't. That's another whole set of interesting ethical issues for another book.

ONLY IN AMERICA DOES "IT MIGHT WORK" WORK

But even if you take those provider financial motivation issues out of the equation, and just look at the question of how much money should we spend on experimental care for a dying patient with no conventional care alternative, that truly is a very hard issue to resolve. It is an issue society should openly discuss and collectively solve. How much money should be spent on highly problematic and unproven care is a much tougher issue to resolve when that totally experimental care is the patient's "only hope" — particularly when there is no good science underlying that hope.

What we do know about experimental care in America is that we are the only country in the world where "it might work" is grounds for a benefit payment in any care setting other than a limited set of carefully structured and carefully supervised clinical trials.

The simple fact that a new medical procedure or device is still in purely "experimental" status absolutely stops and freezes payments in most other countries for all care outside of very well-structured and closely supervised clinical trials.

That point is relevant to the question of why care costs in America go up faster than the general rate of inflation. That major difference in the approach to paying for unproven, untested, and experimental care is one reason that health care costs in the United States go up faster than in many European nations and why care costs go up faster than the rate of inflation.[19]

In most purchase situations, we get what we pay for. In these kinds of experimental care cases, the formula is reversed and we pay for what we get, whether or not it has value.

Based on the easy to verify experience of every other country where the government itself does get involved in those discussions and payment decisions, much tougher standards are applied to experimental care coverage when the government is the payer. Likewise, Medicare and Medicaid — our own government care programs — each have very clear payment exclusions for purely experimental care. Only private insurers in America ever cover experimental care.

The big cost drivers are not experimental care. The major cost drivers are new and "proven" items of care. As a general rule and as a general practice, functional, nonexperimental, high-tech, and high-cost care innovations are funded and paid for far more fully, more quickly, and more richly in America than anywhere in the world. Pharmaceutical companies and medical technology companies from many countries definitely rely on America as the foundation and basic cash source for a very high proportion of their product development income.

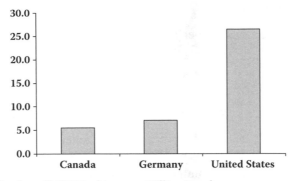

Figure 2.3   Number of MRI Machines per Million People

And because so many new things are now covered, the cost of care in America goes up at a rate that significantly exceeds that normal rate of inflation.

The result of that specific, fairly lush cash flow can be seen pretty easily in the health care business model and operational infrastructure of American health care.

We do more MRI, CT, and high-tech diagnostic scans in America than anywhere in the world.[20] (See Figure 2.3.) The good news is that those scans often produce wonderful, almost miraculous images. The bad news is that those scans usually cost more money than the technologies they are replacing or supplementing. And, because they are both profitable and easily available, we now do a lot more of them. So care is often better and total costs very consistently go up.

Drug costs in the United States are, on average, 2.3 times more expensive than the same drugs in the rest of the world. America spends 54 percent more than other countries on the top five inpatient devices — defibrillators, pacemakers, coronary stents, hip implants, and knee implants.[21] Prices per unit are much higher in the United States — and those prices are going up every year.[22]

Care improvements are a good thing. Better hips and better knee implants are good things. Single-beam lasers that can explode a single cancer cell are good things. New technology isn't bad. New technology can perform miracles — make our lives better and improve our functionality — so we absolutely do not want to stop progress. We just need to do a better job of measuring the real value of each piece of progress, and we need to know how much it costs because we all pay in our taxes or our premiums for each piece of progress.

LET'S REQUIRE DISCLOSURE OF EFFECTIVENESS RESEARCH

The government now requires all companies who advertise drugs to be very explicit in describing every possible complication of the drug in their ads. We've all heard those ads on the TV and radio. At the same time, strangely, the government does not require the drug companies to talk at all about their actual research-based data showing the likely relative impact of a drug. So the ads and the patient disclosure materials can be completely silent about the fact that the research for a particular new drug showed clearly that the new drug doesn't actually save anyone's life — but the drug does, on average, prolong life for certain cancer patients by one month or less. Or less than six months. The research people know that number. Each drug comes with a likely impact. The drug companies know what that impact is. They, however, tend not to share that knowledge with the patient using the drug. That isn't right. Consumers should know that data.

We need to expand the disclosure requirements for those expensive new treatments so patients know exactly what each new treatment is shown by research to do. Patients deserve to know and manufacturers should be forced to disclose. Their current database could be used. The FDA could help each drug manufacturer script that patient disclosure document for each new drug treatment.

People often take new drugs hoping to be cured — when the actual drug company research showed clearly that the mortality results for the patient of taking or not taking the drugs are exactly the same.

In any case, the cost of new drugs, new treatments, new technologies, new tests, and new procedures are constantly driving up the cost of care in America faster than the simple rate of inflation.

MASSIVE CARE COORDINATION DEFICIENCIES ADD EXPENSES

If those were the only cost drivers for health care, we would probably find the total rate of cost increases in this country painful but affordable. The fourth cost driver is a bit more of a challenge. Line four is the growing array of costs and the increasing levels of waste and inefficiency that

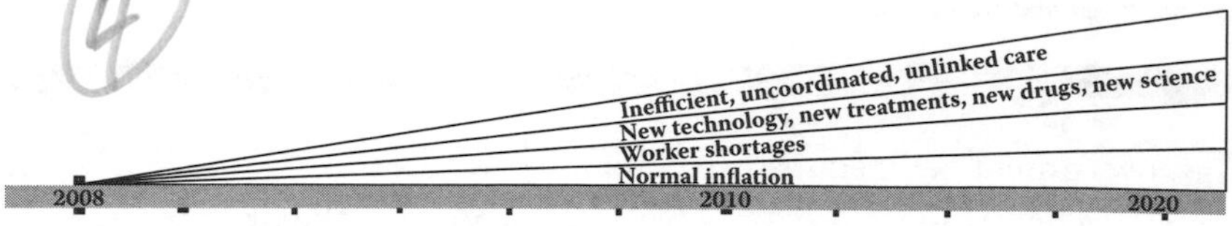

Figure 2.4   Cost Drivers — American Health Care

result from the almost complete lack of coordination between American caregivers. (See Figure 2.4.) Why do we care if most U.S. caregivers don't coordinate care very well with each other? The most expensive patients in America tend to be the ones with co-morbidities. Americans with co-morbidities — multiple care conditions — almost always have at least one separate medical specialist for each separate medical condition. Those separate caregivers all want to do the right thing for their patients but those unconnected specialty caregivers typically do not coordinate care with one another for very many, if any, of their patients.

MULTIPLE CAREGIVERS DON'T LINK WELL

Ask anyone with multiple health conditions if that is true. Ask anyone trying to coordinate care for an aging parent if that is true. In most care settings, the lack of information sharing and care coordination between caregivers is so inadequate that it verges on scandalous. We have, as a result, massive care linkage deficiencies in American health care, and large numbers of patients suffer as a result.

That problem might be understandable and even acceptable for us as a nation if only a small portion of the total health care economy involved the direct care of patients with co-morbidities. But the facts are pretty clear that over two-thirds of all the health care dollars spent in America are spent on patients with co-morbidities, and we are seeing regular growth in the numbers of those patients.

We do not link care well for those patients. Major inefficiencies and unnecessary expenses result. Basic care delivery inefficiencies and chronic care linkage deficiencies drive a significant portion of health care costs — and the number of patients with co-morbidities who need coordinated care is climbing regularly.[23] Good research shows that spending for a patient with one chronic condition is about a few times the average cost of a patient

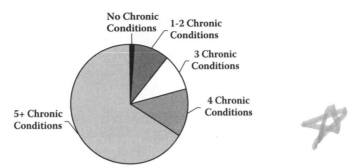

Figure 2.5   Percentage of Medicare Spending by Number of Chronic Conditions

with no chronic conditions, and spending is 25 times greater for a patient with five or more chronic conditions.[24] (See Figure 2.5.)

We obviously need tools to help physicians link up better with each other and with their patients. Those tools will be discussed later in the book. Until we have them in place, care linkage deficiencies will drive up the costs of care in America faster than the rate of inflation.

PERVERSE FINANCIAL INCENTIVES ALSO INCREASE COSTS

The fifth major cost driver for American health care is one that anyone with the most fundamental grasp of basic elementary economics should see instantly as a problem: As noted earlier in this book, most of our care providers unfortunately have very perverse direct financial incentives relative to both care improvement and care coordination.

Health care in America is almost entirely a piecework industry. Providers in this country make their living selling pieces of care rather than packages of care. The economic model of American health care is structured around separate caregivers selling individual care procedures by the individual unit.

Chapter 1 noted that there are more than 18,000 billing codes for individual care procedures in America. There are zero billing codes for either care improvement or an actual cure. Zero. Health care providers in every country on the planet do what they are paid to do by the revenue stream of that country.

That is not a critical comment. It's a pure economic observation and it is a basic economic reality. Selling what the customer buys is how economic units in any industry and any market always function. Vendors in any given market both produce and sell exactly what and only what the customers in that market actually pay for and buy. Anything that isn't bought simply isn't produced. How many black and white TV sets do we see in stores today?

In American health care, procedures are what customers buy, so we have a lot of procedures. Care linkages are not a billable procedure, so care linkages typically do not happen. Preventing a major heart attack is not a billable event, so prevention tends to be haphazard, sporadic, uncoordinated, and, at best, marginally effective. An asthma crisis can generate a $10,000 to $30,000 billable event per patient for the involved caregivers. Asthma prevention services generate, at best, a very small fee.

The real irony is, fully successful prevention of a painful, terrifying, life-threatening, and high-cost asthma crisis generates no fee at all.

So the highest value and most desirable outcome for an asthma patient generates no revenue at all for the total care infrastructure. And — even more perversely — the lowest value, least desirable, most costly, and obviously most damaging outcome creates huge provider revenue flows and almost always results in significant provider profit.

That is a bizarre set of economic incentives when you think about it. And, as is true of any economic system, we almost always get exactly what we incent. No one should be surprised by that outcome.

PROBLEMATIC INSURANCE BENEFIT DESIGN

The somewhat problematic design of our insurance coverage benefit plans often makes that whole economic situation worse. The structure of insurance plans usually insulate consumers from dealing directly with the actual costs of care. That creates one set of problems. That set of issues is compounded by the fact that a typical fixed deductible insurance package basically also insulates all high-cost providers from any direct negative impact when they raise their charges or fees.

In fact, consumers are usually so insulated from the direct impact of fee levels that they sometimes criticize their health plans when the plans try to negotiate or pay lower fees to the providers of care.

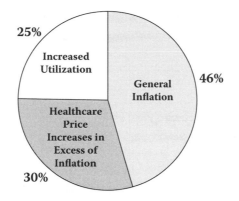

Source: The Factors Fueling Rising Healthcare Costs, PriceWaterhouseCoopers, 2008

Figure 2.6   Factors Contributing to Health Care Insurance Premium Increases

Health plans and insurers do try to negotiate rates for the people they cover, and there are some successes in that area. But it's a challenging battle. As you can see from the chart below, 75 percent of the cost increases in care in America last year came from higher prices per unit of care — not higher volumes of care. (See Figure 2.6.) Monopoly or oligopoly caregivers tend to have major negotiating leverage in quite a few geographic areas. Medicare and Medicaid simply set their own fees by dictate, so they always pay less then everyone else. There are always negotiations going on between plans, insurers, and caregivers on fees.

Care prices would be a lot higher if those negotiations were not happening. But fees still go up, and because of the way insurance benefit packages are designed, the actual fee increases by health care providers are almost always invisible to individual consumers.

No one with a good grasp of basic economics would ever design that fee-based, piecework, uncoordinated, volume-incented, consumer-insulated payment system from scratch if the goal of the whole purchasing process at any level was to improve care quality, create care delivery efficiency, empower informed consumer care purchasing, or positively impact the total costs of care.

So why do we have such a strange system? It is an artifact of history. It is how Americans have always purchased care, by the piece. That model just happened — rather than being designed by the market or set up deliberately by care delivery buyers and customers. It has survived because it is easy to administer, it creates huge revenue flows, and our current infrastructure of care is built almost entirely on the massive revenue stream it creates. So it has great momentum.

CHANGES IN FEE PAYMENT APPROACHES FACE RESISTANCE

Many providers love the current payment system. That should not surprise anyone. Follow the dollars. Two point five trillion dollars. Most current American health care providers make a significant amount of money with their current fees and current payment approaches. Large numbers of providers are very fond of receiving fees ... and, to be fair, most American health care providers must depend entirely on fees to make their living. So any proposal or economic model that threatens fees as a free-flowing revenue stream for American caregivers very directly and personally threatens their livelihood and maybe even their economic survival.

Every independent economic unit in any industry tends to defend its own livelihood. So a fee-based system naturally creates its own significant barriers to change and will not voluntarily self-correct. Health plans tried to bring down the total cost of care in America by reducing "unnecessary" hospital days. A decade ago, it was not uncommon for patients to be admitted to the hospital on Friday for Monday surgery. Maternity lengths of stay averaged a week. Health plans took steps to bring down the length of stay to "medically appropriate" days — and had some successes. In some cases, those efforts to reduce unnecessary care costs created a patient backlash, and health plans stopped some programs to reduce lengths of stay.

But hospital lengths of stay and admission levels did go down some as a result of those efforts. Hospitals responded to the reduction in admission rates and length of stay by simply increasing the cost per admission. Figure 2.7 shows the relative amount of money spent on each category of care.

Hospitals' costs were relatively flat for a couple of years, and then began to spike up as hospitals learned how to charge for more services for each patient. Figure 2.8 shows the rate of increase in cost per hospital patient over the past six years.

American hospitals are quite good at generating revenue. Figure 2.9 shows the comparative cost per day in American, French, Canadian, and Japanese hospitals. Notice any patterns to the spending?

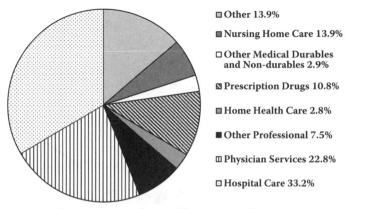

- ▣ Other 13.9%
- ▣ Nursing Home Care 13.9%
- ▢ Other Medical Durables and Non-durables 2.9%
- ▣ Prescription Drugs 10.8%
- ▣ Home Health Care 2.8%
- ■ Other Professional 7.5%
- ▥ Physician Services 22.8%
- ▢ Hospital Care 33.2%

Figure 2.7   National Expenditures for Health Service and Supplies by Category, 1980 and 2007

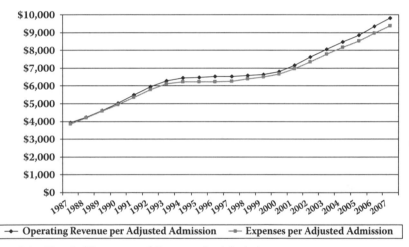

◆ Operating Revenue per Adjusted Admission   ■ Expenses per Adjusted Admission

Figure 2.8   Hospital Revenue and Expenses by Admission

Figure 2.10 shows another interesting point of comparison. The per-capita cost of physician care in America is clearly the highest in the world. Yet American patients have fewer visits to physicians than patients in comparable countries. So the cost drivers are clearly not volumes of visits but price per visit. Any comparison of American health care costs with the rest of the world needs to look at those relationships.

Provider fees and care costs in America go up faster than inflation because provider fees are not subject to very many real market forces in this country. Providers benefit directly by increasing the volume of services provided by each provider to each patient, and very few providers face any negative consequences from consumers for price increases. In

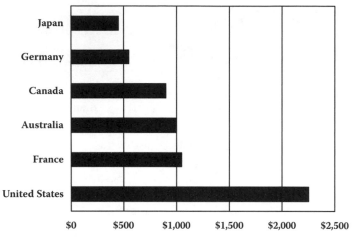

Figure 2.9   Adjusted Cost per Hospital Day

When we compare physician costs in the U.S. to a number of other countries, we see that per-capita spending on physician visits is higher in the U.S., but the number of physician visits per capita is lower.

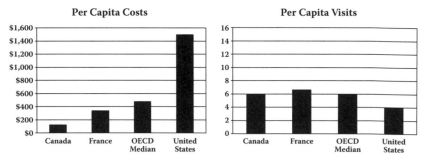

Figure 2.10   Physician Visits/Physician Costs

some cases, state attorney generals have actually stepped in to protect and reinforce high provider fees when payers have attempted to bring them to "reasonable" levels. It's a miracle that fees in America aren't a lot higher than they are.

WE ARE GETTING OLDER AND MORE EXPENSIVE

Those do not comprise, however, the entire package of cost drivers. There is one more major and extremely important cost driver that we also all need to recognize and understand: getting old. The sixth major cost driver

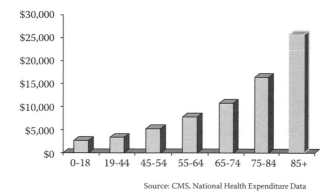

Source: CMS, National Health Expenditure Data

Figure 2.11   Per Capita Annualized Health Care Costs by Age Group

for American health care is our aging population. Simple survival by large numbers of people is also a huge and growing cost factor for American health care.

Again, the facts are pretty obvious and very hard to challenge. We are getting older as a nation. That is economically relevant because the average annual cost of care for an 18 year old is "only" $2,650. For a 40 year old, the average cost increases to $3,370. For a 65 year old, the average annual cost is up to $10,778. And for an 85 year old, the annual cost of care now runs roughly $25,691 per person.[25] That's about 10 times more expensive than the care used by an average 18 year old. Ten times is a lot of expense.

Look at the aging American cost chart (Figure 2.11). Those obviously are not minor differences in expense levels. Aging is a major cost driver for American health care. The baby boomers are getting older. We will see an additional nine million Americans cross into their 60s over the next five years.[26] Total costs in this country will be affected accordingly. The need for caregivers and care facilities will, of course, also increase. That will, all by itself, add an additional level of expense because health care wages will need to increase even more to alleviate an even greater worker shortage.

Aging is a very good thing. We definitely encourage aging. We don't want to end or limit aging. But we do need to look very hard at how we can target and mitigate the current medical cost impacts of aging and, when we ask ourselves why health care costs go up faster than the rate of normal inflation, we all need to recognize the fact that an aging American population will, all by itself, drive the costs of care significantly higher than pure and simple inflation (see Figure 2.12).

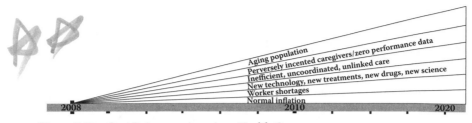

Figure 2.12   Cost Drivers — American Health Care

INFLATION, TECHNOLOGY, INEFFICIENCY, PERVERSE INCENTIVES, AND GETTING OLD ARE AN EXPENSIVE PACKAGE

So that's the combined package of factors that primarily drives health care cost increases in America: basic inflation, health care worker shortages, badly organized and un-coordinated care, badly designed benefit packages, perversely incented care, care sold by the piece and not by the package, an aging population, significant and frequent technological and scientific enhancements, and expensive (but often very effective and much appreciated) improvements in some of the more important, expensive, and generally useful aspects and tools of care.

If we really want to make care affordable in this country, we need to look directly and hard at the most significant, highest leverage, major cost drivers for American health care. We also need to directly face the fact that care is unaffordable for too many Americans because we simply don't do major aspects of care delivery very well or very efficiently.

AS A PURE, SELF-SERVING SYSTEM — HEALTH CARE IS WINNING

A basic set of very powerful economic realities are now at play in American health care. We all very much need to keep in mind that the current total reward system in this country for health care providers and technology manufacturers has created the most profitable and fastest growing health care infrastructure in the world.

If the American automobile industry had the same economic momentum, revenue stream, growth rate, and profit margin as health care, we would immediately declare automobile manufacturing to be the best industry in America — maybe the best in the world.

As noted in Chapter 1, it would be a bit naïve at this point to expect that an economically victorious nonsystem that currently is generating well over $2.5 trillion in annual aggregate revenue will somehow magically, spontaneously, or altruistically reform itself. The current perverse financial incentives embedded deeply in our health care economy combine to very directly drive up the total cost of care for America for the simple reason that almost all health care cost increases are profitable for the people and companies who increase the costs, and there are almost no negative market consequences for raising prices.

CONSUMERS PAY THE PRICE FOR MORE EXPENSIVE CARE

So what happens when care costs go up in America? Who ends up paying for the higher cost of care? Basically, when the smoke clears on that issue, there are actually only two baseline, ultimate payers who pay for all increases in health care costs. The two ultimate payers are the consumer and the taxpayer.

How do those two bottom line payers pay? Usually through (1) premium increases and (2) government program funding.

Government programs are funded through tax dollars. Or debt. Non-government care costs are translated to consumers in the United States most often and most directly through their health coverage premiums. When health care costs go up, health care premium costs go up proportionally.

For governmentally insured patients, the governmental budgets and spend rates for care-related government programs go up as well, dollar for dollar. Each new Medicare care expense immediately becomes a new Medicare budget expense. Each new private insurance care expense immediately becomes an insurance premium increase.

CARE COSTS CREATE PREMIUM COSTS

An amazing number of people do not recognize the direct relationship between increasing care costs and increasing health care premiums. It's actually a very simple and very direct relationship. Care costs create premium costs. For the privately insured population in America the basic economic model is this: The total and actual costs of care each year are simply added up by each health insurer for the people in each insurance "risk pool" and then those costs are divided by the number of insured people in each risk pool to calculate and create the premium that is then charged to the people who buy that specific private insurance coverage. It's basic arithmetic. So when a new procedure or device is added to the care delivery arsenal and it becomes a "covered benefit," the actual cost of that device is simply added proportionately to each insured person's premium. Everyone with insurance pays a piece of each new cost.

The arithmetic is pretty simple and pretty immediate. Care costs create premium costs. So as health care costs go up faster than inflation, for all of the reasons described earlier in this chapter, health care premiums go up by that same percentage to pay the new costs. When hospitals raise their costs per patient by the amounts shown in Figure 2.9, those costs go directly to the premium paid by each insured person. Hospital price increases create premium price increases. Premium is the only possible source of the monies needed to pay hospitals. And the doctors. And the pharmaceutical manufacturers.

Government programs, of course, pay the additional costs of new drugs, new technology, and new care from the Medicare trust fund or from direct state and federal tax dollars, or from some form of government borrowing.

"PASS THROUGH" TO THE CUSTOMER

It's all a pass-through situation. So America has an economic system that provides billions of dollars in cash flow to the companies that invent, sell, and distribute new drugs, new tests, new treatments, and new procedures, and the total costs of those new approaches are simply added to the total cost of health care premiums and taxes in America on a regular and growing basis — at levels that significantly exceed the basic cost of core routine business cost inflation in America. See Figure 2.3 for the relative number of MRI machines in the United States and Canada. That's a useful ratio to keep in mind when asking why health care costs and health care premiums in America go up at a rate that exceeds general inflation.

Why does Canada have fewer MRIs? In Canada, the taxpayers buy each MRI machine through their taxes and Canadian citizens don't like tax increases, so relatively few expensive machines are purchased. Those machines are purely a fixed expense item for Canadian caregivers — not a revenue source. In the United States, we buy care by the piece. That means that each machine creates a per-patient flow of cash for the caregiver who owns the machine. So quite a few American caregivers buy those machines, and they get used quite often.

Those current financial realities need to be addressed as part of the overall public discussions of health care costs. The final chapter of this book calls for a full and complete public disclosure and discussion of all health care costs and all health care cost drivers. We need everyone in America to understand both health care costs and the American health care infrastructure.

THE ANSWER IS "RIGHT CARE"

The good news is that there are very good cost mitigators that we can use to reduce the cost of care in America. The Rand study, Wennberg studies, and the Commonwealth studies cited earlier in this book all point to the fact that delivering care more effectively and consistently can reduce the cost of care. We can obviously do a much better job of delivering care. In this country, if we just reform a few basic elements of care, we should be able take steps to cut the number of kidney failures in half.[27] We should also be able to cut the number of people who become diabetic by half,[28] and we can also reduce blindness, amputations, and organ failures significantly for the people who do become diabetic.[29] John Wennberg's data shows that we could save Medicare from a cost perspective by simply having the best performing areas of the country become the standard for care and cost for the rest of the country. And we all know that even the best performing areas of the country could deliver better care.

The answer is "right" care. Better care is the only good path we have out of this mess.

It's a good time to start down that path. We should start by setting a few very important goals to get us all focused, and then we could put some programs in place to achieve those goals. Until then, care costs will continue to go up at a rate that significantly exceeds the general rate of inflation in America.

3

Set Goals and Improve Care

Most people believe that caregivers have constant access to the most current scientific data about care, and that caregivers in this country consistently use that information in systematic, coordinated, and collaborative ways to make care better for patients in America.

Most people are wrong. There is a huge amount of variation in health care delivery in America today, and very little of that variation is based on either medical science or collaborative efforts to improve care.

There is a lot of good evidence showing how unsystematic, inconsistent, and even dangerous the variations in American health care are. One study took 135 doctors and gave all of the doctors the same patient. The doctors came up with 82 different treatments.[1]

The rate of tonsillectomies for children in two adjacent communities can vary from 20 percent in one community to 70 percent in the adjacent community.[2] The rate of heart by-pass surgery can vary by 200 percent between directly adjacent communities ... and between two hospitals in the same community.[3]

Within the exact same hospital, the patterns of care for a given medical condition can vary by more than 80 percent — from the highest utilization doctor to the lowest utilization doctor — for patients with identical conditions.

One study showed that the 60-day patient mortality rate for cancer surgery ranged from a low of 5.4 percent to a high of 12.3 percent depending on the caregiver who did the surgery.[4] Another study showed that radiologists have very different success levels in detecting cancer using mammograms, and the highest scoring and most skillful radiologists caught 76 percent more breast cancers than the lower scoring radiologists.[5]

So the people who believe that a surgeon is a surgeon, and a radiologist is a radiologist, should know about the numbers that various studies have uncovered about the very real differences in performance that can exist between caregivers. Most Americans do not know or even suspect that these differences exist.

Most patients actually have a simple faith that their own caregiver is at the top of the outcome scale when it comes to both skill and effectiveness. That obviously can't always be true. Most people also believe incorrectly that American caregivers as a group have an overarching strategic direction and an actual operational agenda targeted at continuously improving both the quality and outcomes of care.

The truth is that there is no overarching agenda for care improvement in America. There are, in fact, very few local care improvement agendas. The ones that do exist are almost always very limited in scope. Many caregivers do engage in individual quality improvement projects of one kind or another, but the caregiver-based projects that do exist are always very local, very specific, very narrow, and very rarely transferable or transferred to any other site.

It's worse than you think. Usually quality improvement projects that happen on one floor of a hospital don't even transfer to other floors of that same hospital. Unless you have actually worked in a hospital, that level of inconsistency is almost impossible to believe or comprehend. Processes as simple as the transfer of key and specific medical information about individual patients from nurse to nurse in the actual care setting at the end of each shift can vary within a hospital from department to department and floor to floor — and can vary even within the same department from shift to shift and nurse to nurse. Mistakes are made, patients are damaged, and additional care costs are created by those all too common levels of pervasive process inconsistency and unmeasured, unmonitored, and unmanaged data transfer and data recording mistakes and errors.

Most hospitals don't even have well-trained "Rapid Response Teams" set up to deal with crisis patients who are in imminent risk of dying quickly. In far too many settings, those response teams invent themselves on the fly when a patient is in danger of dying, and the approaches actually used to save the patient and deliver needed care can change from shift to shift and patient to patient based on which caregivers happen to be working in that area at that time.

The best care sites run crisis simulations and drills and have clear procedures for "Code Blue" patients. Many more sites just respond in the moment and the caregivers on the scene at that moment do what they can with the supplies, coworkers, and care resources available. Inconsistent crisis responses happen all the time and patients suffer. Patients in America have no idea that the consistency levels or process engineering levels in broad areas of health care at many care sites are so stunningly low.

Information transfer mistakes are common. Medication errors of one kind or another also happen with frightening regularity, in part due to a frequent lack of systematic thinking about the care process issues that relate to accurate medication delivery and verification.

One recent study of patients admitted to six Massachusetts hospitals showed that there were so many medication errors that one out of ten patients routinely suffered a "preventable adverse drug event."[6] That's a lot of errors. The hospitals involved in the study had no clue that so many patients were being routinely damaged until the study was done.

Computerized order entry for prescription drugs in those hospitals would probably have prevented most of those adverse events. This type of mistake and care inconsistency does not have to happen. Tools are available to make sure that those kinds of adverse events do not happen.

The sad and scary truth, however, is that health care typically does not engineer or re-engineer a lot of very basic processes, and health care doesn't learn from itself in any consistent way. It's sometimes almost institutional eccentricity. Most other industries use confidentiality agreements that keep key employees who change employers from taking new ideas or valuable process improvement learnings to competitors when competitors hire them. Health care actually doesn't make people sign those agreements because, as a rule, no one in health care consistently learns from anyone else, and there is so little process improvement going on in most care settings that people who really do bring great new ideas from an old employer to a new care team are often simply told, "Well, hey — that's not how we do that here. We do what we do. We do what we have always done. If you liked their approach so much, you should have stayed there."

DATA ISN'T SHARED

Data sharing is almost unknown in most areas of health care. People from other industries are often stunned when they learn how little process learning or data sharing goes on in most care settings.

Most care sites have little or no data. The individual health care business entities that do have data generally keep their own data to themselves. A few large and progressive care systems are beginning to share data internally and with each other — and that is a very good thing — but apples-to-apples comparing of data across various care sites is almost unknown. In some communities, it doesn't happen at all.

As noted earlier, multiple studies have shown that there are actually huge variations in care delivery performance levels between sites, providers, care systems, and care teams. Reading mammograms is a good example. Most patients have no clue that not all mammographers read mammograms with the same level of accuracy and skill. Women tend to feel protected just because a mammogram was done. The truth is, depending on who may have read their mammogram, women can be more than twice as likely to end up with late stage breast cancer simply because their early stage cancers were completely undetected when their mammogram was read. Mammography interpretation skills vary significantly. So do surgical outcomes, as do actual survival rates from various care teams for various procedures and conditions.

Survival rates from oncologists can vary significantly. But, again, patients today have no way of knowing which oncologist or knee surgeon or heart surgeon or mammographer to pick based on proven results or quantifiable data.

Even more alarming, the knee surgeons and oncologists and mammographers who have the worst outcomes have no way of knowing that their own care outcomes are not as good as they could or should be. So those key caregivers can't get better, based on knowing that the performance problem exists.

All doctors are "A" students. All doctors want to be the best. All doctors want to deliver great care to their patients. But doctors generally don't have the data they need to be in a continuous improvement modality. Only a few large multispecialty group practices have any of those kinds of programs in place.

The Institute of Medicine currently has an active task force targeted at improving the degree that evidence-based care is used as the standard of care in America. The current goal is to have 90 percent of care based on evidence by the year 2020. Think about how sad that goal is. It says we need to take an entire decade to get to the point where 90 percent of care in the richest care system in the world is based on medical evidence. We need to do a lot better than that.

RANDOM TOOLS CREATE RANDOM RESULTS

We need consistent best practices, and we need higher quality of care in America. Simply hoping that caregivers will get better is not our best plan. That hasn't worked so far. Doing a bunch of random, nontransferable, site-specific, narrow-scope, one-off, local quality improvement projects is also not our best plan.

Trying to add one or more random tools to the care improvement environment in the vague hopes a new tool might somehow do some good for some people is also not our best plan.

So what should we do to improve care?

BEGIN WITH GOALS

We should set real targets for care improvement in a small number of very large and important areas, and then we should actually put programs and processes and tools in place to improve that care and achieve those goals.

Goals are the key. One of the very few care improvement initiatives that has had a positive impact on the quality of care in America is the Institute for Health Care Improvement "100,000 Lives" campaign. That campaign set a goal of saving lives through several specific techniques, and the program influenced caregivers all over America. More than 100,000 lives were saved. We are all in Don Berwick's debt. That campaign stands alone, but it does prove that a program founded on goals and supported by strategy can work in American health care.

Starting with goals could make a huge difference in the cost and quality of care, because the goals give us an intellectual context to figure out what needs to be changed and what needs to be done.

Goals are, in fact, essential for building successful care improvement strategies. We can't really design systematic care improvement processes until we are very clear on exactly what care we want to improve. Simply saying we want care to be better for people with asthma doesn't point us toward any particular activity. Saying that we will cut the number of severe asthma crises in half in two years does, however, point us in very real direction — and it gives us real things to do to achieve that goal.

WE DON'T NEED A THOUSAND GOALS

We don't need to set a thousand goals for a thousand different care conditions to make a huge difference in care delivery. Five conditions create well over half of our total health care costs.[7] We could start with roughly six key goals relevant to those specific conditions and work from there.

If we start with a very specific goal like cutting asthma attacks in half, or cutting kidney failures in half, or in the future for an acute care condition doubling the life expectancy of stage three breast cancer patients — then we can work backward from the goal to create a strategy. And we can work backward from the strategy to create and implement the real world tools needed to achieve each of the goals.

Starting with a real goal allows creative, practical, operations-focused problem-solving caregivers to work backward from the specific target to figure out the functional steps needed to make that goal a reality. Goals also allow multiple levels of caregivers to work as a team because all of the caregivers will have a clear sense of the actual care improvement outcome that is being collectively pursued.

Goal setting also can mobilize the patients, both to get their support for the goals and to help guide patients' decisions about key elements of their own care and their own activities. Goals have good uses at multiple levels with multiple stakeholders.

WORK BACKWARD FROM THE GOAL TO THE STRATEGY

This is a breathtakingly practical and simple approach to care improvement. Take asthma as an example. Asthma is one of the six most expensive chronic conditions. It is the most prevalent disease among American children. It is the fastest growing disease in America for children.[8] Asthma care in America today tends to be inconsistent and it is very often ineffective. At least half of the painful, frightening, and extremely expensive hospital admissions for asthma patients could be eliminated if asthma care were better.[9]

So what exactly should the specific asthma care improvement goal be? It's pretty ineffective to set a vaguely generic goal like, "making asthma care better." That's hard to describe and it's hard to measure. "Better" doesn't create any sense of magnitude, or of needed creativity. Little goals generate little incremental plans. Generic goals generate minimal specificity relative to action steps. Big goals, however, can generate major innovations and trigger real creative thinking. We need big goals. Real, meaningful, relevant, and big.

So what would a big asthma goal be? We need a goal that is measurable, focusing, definitive, aligning, and inspirational — so that we will all feel good when it gets done. What can we measure about asthma care? We all know that if asthma care fails for a given patient and a hospital admission ensues for that patient, that is a bad thing. A hospital admission for an asthma patient is usually a clear failure of prehospital care for that specific patient. The admission itself is measurable. It's real. It's easy to count and easy to explain. So to focus our planning on asthma care improvement across the full spectrum of care, we could start with a clear, quantifiable, highly directional goal that simply says, "Our goal is to cut the number of crisis-level hospital admissions needed for our asthma patients in half in two years."

Half is a big number. It reeks of magnitude. It calls for action. We can't cut the asthma admissions in half by sending out memos. Care would need to be better in many care sites to achieve that goal. Logic, experience, and medical science all tell us that we would have to improve asthma care in quite a few ways and quite a few places to achieve that outcome. Cutting crises in half isn't a mere "process" measure — like "giving 80 percent of asthma patients an educational brochure by year end." It's a real outcome measure and the outcome it measures can't be achieved unless we make front end asthma care better for a lot of people.

It's also a goal that is so clear-cut that lay people and caregivers can both understand it and have a sense that it's a really good thing to achieve.

How would that goal be used? That's the beauty of a clear goal. If we decide to set the very basic goal of cutting serious asthma crises in half for an entire population in a given time frame, then we can start from that very basic goal and ask ourselves the very practical real world question: How in the world do we actually do that?

Going from a goal to a plan is obviously a very different approach from the current American health improvement nonstrategy of simply hoping that each of the doctors who treat asthma patients in a given community will somehow independently figure out how they can improve care in some way for some or all of their asthma patients. Simply hoping asthma care will get better absolutely will not reduce the number of asthma crises by 50 percent. Nor will sending out various kinds of notes and memos and brochures to lots of people about asthma care. Notes and memos can be very nicely done, but they tend to have limited impact. Who reads notes? Think about how care delivery really works. The doctors who take care of asthma patients are all busy. Very busy. They don't have time to read a lot of notes. They also don't have the time or the resources or very many of the tools needed to systematically improve asthma care, and, in the real world, those busy caregivers will not somehow create those tools or connect with other doctors or with the local emergency room because someone sent them a memo or note explaining that it is a good idea.

The odds of a memo being read are small and the odds of a doctor changing practice after reading a memo on asthma care are even smaller — unless the memo outlines a wonderful brand new cure that isn't currently known to the doctor and the note is written by someone the doctor respects as an absolute authority on asthma care. That doesn't happen very often.

Remember how American health care is organized. Or disorganized. Doctors are usually functional and economic silos — each working on their own — typically seeing their own patients on an individual basis and getting paid only when patients get sick and come to them for care.

We know from good research that less than half of the children with asthma in that nonorganized care environment are getting right care now.[10] That tells us that the opportunity for asthma care improvement can be huge if we get the care nonsystem to perform more efficiently and effectively.

How do we do that? We need a plan. We need a plan that brings consistent information about better asthma care to all asthma patients and to all of the caregivers involved in asthma care.

We need a functional strategy to systematically improve asthma care in the context of a nonsystem care infrastructure. To build that strategy, we need to think in very practical terms about asthma care and the real world processes, tools, and steps needed to achieve our specific goal of cutting the number of major asthma crises in half.

What is the first step? Diagnosing asthma is a good place to start. It's immediately obvious that a first step in that strategy needs to be to find out who has asthma. That's pretty basic logic. We can't deliver better care to patients with asthma if we don't know who they are. Practicality rules. We need to know who has asthma.

How can we find out who has asthma? Again, we can't simply hope that widespread and consistent diagnosis of all asthma cases will magically happen. Hope is good but we already know it is insufficient to improve care.

We need a plan and a process. Processes become relevant when goals exist. We know that we need to develop a practical process for each relevant population that results in every asthmatic in a targeted community being detected and diagnosed. Those detection and diagnosis plans can and will vary a bit from community to community and care site to care site, but it is a very doable task — and we can make asthma detection a priority for all relevant care sites. We can set up a process for doctors in a given community or setting to diagnose all asthmatics in their patient population in a given time frame. To prime the data pump, we can use the database of the insurance companies who pay claims for every insured child and use that information to provide feedback to the relevant caregivers and to each child's parent. It is very possible to design a process to achieve that goal of identifying all asthmatics if we begin with the goal and then think in practical terms in the context of each community and relevant population about how to achieve it.

We need to make the decision to have all relevant caregivers in each area trained on asthma diagnosis. That type of communitywide training for a particular health care condition currently is never done except in the case of possible pandemics. But it is an absolutely possible thing to do if we simply decide collectively as community leaders and major health care purchasers to do it and then assign someone to do it. There is a finite number of relevant caregivers in every community. So we can figure out ways for that learning process to happen and for that diagnostic work to be done for that specific condition for whatever population we choose to target in each community in America. Remember — we can't be setting goals for a thousand conditions. We need to set just a few major goals so we can put a few major agendas in place. For asthma, the agenda needs to involve all of the key caregivers in each community who treat asthma patients. They all need to be contacted.

Several physician contact tools and mechanisms already exist. We need to use those tools to connect our caregivers and reach out to our patients. Health plans, public health agencies, relevant hospitals, and special task forces or project-focused agencies set up to do that work or something similar could all get that job of physician focus on asthma done.

In many respects, health plans might be the easiest mechanism to use quickly since health plans all have contracted provider networks, provider listings, and in-place mechanisms to contract providers. Building some of that existing functionality and contact capability from scratch is entirely possible but it can be more difficult to do and take longer. Since the current provider networks for most health plans and most government agencies already overlap almost entirely in most settings, we don't need every plan to notify each provider separately. A collaborative effort would not be difficult to set up. We can ensure that at least one payer notifies each provider in a community about the asthma agenda and needed next steps for asthma care.

In any case, if we really believe and decide that we need to contact all relevant providers in each targeted community in order to cut asthma crises in half, we then need to look at the array of options available to us in each geographic area and we need to pick the provider communication strategy package that works best for each area. Buyers can play a key role in that process by simply demanding that this work be done. Health plans that function in those geographic areas can be and should be asked to do that asthma strategy implementation work by every buyer. Physicians can also be asked to do that work by every payer, including Medicare and Medicaid. Universal coverage for American children will be a huge asset for a communitywide asthma care improvement plan because every child who is covered will be in a government or private payer database, and whoever owns each child's database can do that needed contact work with each child's care provider.

ASTHMA CARE NEEDS COMPUTERIZED DATA

When we think in practical terms about actually cutting the number of crisis-level asthma attacks in half, the second thing we obviously need to do is have the data for every child with asthma on a computer. Why a computer? Paper doesn't cut it for care improvement or care tracking. Paper just sits there. Isolated, unlinked, incomplete, and generally unavailable paper medical records for each child with asthma obviously cannot do the work needed to track asthma care. Only a computer can keep track of the asthma patients and their care. So if we are serious about fixing asthma care in American communities, then we need to be equally serious about getting asthma care data electronically available.

WE NEED COMPUTERIZED ASTHMA CARE DATA

Multiple computer approaches can be used. The computer approach used to put asthma data in electronic files for each child with asthma diagnosis could be an asthma registry, an electronic medical record, or an insurance or Medicaid claims payment database. All of those approaches can work. The functional key is to have an electronic file supporting the care of every asthma patient so we can know at a relevant and actionable level who is and who is not getting the right care.

Once the data for each child with asthma is on a computer, the next practical and logical step is to track care for each asthma patient. Care protocols for asthma exist. This isn't an area where we need a lot of new science. We know a lot about how asthma care should be done. There are therapies, prescriptions, inhalers, group training sessions, breathing exercises, and medical counseling approaches that all work for asthma patients. If we are going to cut the asthma attacks in half, we need to know that each asthma patient has a doctor and that the right levels of care are being delivered.

We need feedback mechanisms about basic care for each child. Right now, doctors who treat asthma patients and write prescriptions for those patients don't even know if their prescriptions are being filled by the children or by their parents.

That is a problem. If prescriptions are written, we need to know if they are actually filled. We need data about children with asthma being screened by easy to use data registries that can tell the doctor if the prescriptions are both filled and then refilled. High percentages of those kinds of prescriptions are not filled now,[11] and the children's caregivers today usually don't have a clue.

Care improvement for asthma needs to be an interactive, patient-focused process. If a child ends up in an emergency room with a crisis-level asthma attack, we need someone to figure out as the accountable member of the care team why the attack happened, and the caregivers involved need to be very sure that appropriate follow-up happens to significantly lower the chance of a future crisis for that child. If no one is accountable, the team will not be able to do its job very well.

In today's care environment, most of the time no one outside the physical crisis point of care even knows which children are having a crisis. And the people at the site of crisis usually don't inform anyone else that a crisis has happened. The emergency room or hospital usually doesn't tell the primary care doctor — if there even is a primary care doctor — that care failed and a hospital was needed by the patient.

Most of the time, no one does any follow-up on the children who have major asthma crises in a hospital emergency room to mitigate the likelihood of a future crisis. That isn't the caregiver's fault. It's a systems failure. A big one. No one usually knows when or where to intervene and help in those cases where a given child is obviously having repeated problems and clearly needs an intervention. Far too many of the children with asthma crises are now uninsured,[12] so today there isn't even a single payer database for these children with their claims-based asthma care information on it.

UNIVERSAL COVERAGE FOR CHILDREN CAN IMPROVE ASTHMA CARE

It's pretty obvious that this whole process of tracking care and improving care would work a lot better if we had universal health coverage for all children, and if we had a longitudinal database for each child based on the insurance claims paid for each child. Many children with asthma are now uninsured and quite a few of those children move from care site to care site. There's often no way today to provide appropriate continuity of either care or medical information. Those children are often almost entirely medically invisible — showing up on the care radar screen only when they are in a state of crisis and disappearing from view as soon as the crisis is over. Not being insured is a huge liability when it comes to longitudinal data and systematic care improvement. Right now, African American children are 40 percent more likely to be uninsured,[13] 1.4 times more likely to have asthma,[14] and 4 times more likely to die from asthma.[15]

That's a very bad combination. Care would be a lot better for those children if they were insured and if there were a longitudinal electronic database about their care available to their caregivers. Universal coverage is a very good idea.

BEING INSURED CREATES A DATABASE

There are a number of other areas of care where there is a clear linkage between not being insured and poor health, and many of those areas relate to chronic conditions.

When you think in practical terms about systematic care improvement agendas for any disease, the functional value of universal coverage becomes very clear very quickly. We need everyone covered with health insurance because we need everyone in the electronic database. Payers — including Medicare and Medicaid — are the only sure short-term source of relatively complete electronic data about American patients at this point in our history. As a starting database for care delivery, and as a major step in reforming care delivery, we should require all payers in America to build a database of comparable, transferable data, and we should require all payers to make that data portable and accessible so we can trigger care registry tools and so the data about each patient can be accessible to all relevant caregivers.

If we set a goal to reduce asthma crises by 50 percent, train all caregivers, track care for all children, and then implement a set of care registry and computer support tools that are used to support the children who have bad cases of asthma, then achieving that goal of cutting asthma crises in half is entirely possible.

CARE WON'T GET BETTER WITHOUT GOALS

But if we don't set the goal — or if we don't create the tools needed to support better care and track care — asthma care will simply not get better.

It may get better in a few sites, but it won't achieve the level of consistent quality care children in America should have when we are spending $2.5 billion on care and when we need to cut the total cost of care in America by reducing avoidable health expenses like crisis-level hospital admissions for asthma.

GOALS FOR KEY DISEASES

We need to set similar goals for other key diseases. Several other important chronic conditions lend themselves very well to very similar outcomes goals. Just like asthma care, the goals we set for each disease can lead to real strategies and the strategies can lead to actual tools. If we say we want to cut the number of kidney failures in half, for example, then the strategies to achieve that goal become equally obvious and the tools needed to support that goal become almost self-evident.

Reducing kidney failures actually is another very good goal. Half the kidney failures in this country should not happen. Kidney failures usually represent a failure of diabetic care. The care improvement strategies and tools needed to cut kidney failures in half have the inherent capability of also improving all care for diabetic patients, ultimately cutting blindness and amputations significantly for diabetic Americans. Cutting kidney failures in half requires a care tool kit focused on specific diabetic patients. Setting that goal allows the tool kit for diabetic care to be designed, created, and implemented.

We need to know collectively what steps need to be taken — both in our payment systems and our care delivery systems — to cut kidney failures in half. Not surprisingly, the key steps for reducing kidney failures look a lot like the steps needed for asthma care. What are those steps? We need to get every potential kidney failure case identified and then recorded in a database that tracks both diagnosis and care. We need the high-risk patients to be supported by care registries and care coordination tools focused on patients with conditions that lend themselves to failed kidneys. Most, but not all, of those patients will be diabetic, so we need a care registry tool kit that supports better care for diabetics with co-morbidities whose kidneys are likely to fail.

Knowing who is at risk is not enough. We need to follow up to monitor each prospective and current case of kidney failure, and we need to insert systematic interventions when the current level or type or effectiveness of care is obviously problematic for a given patient. By being systematic, consistent, and very patient focused, we can cut the number if kidney failures in half, with consistent "right care" as the primary strategy and agenda.

We could also cut the number of heart attacks in half and we could cut the number of congestive heart failure crises in half. We can cut the number of "nonfunctional" days for patients with depression in half. We can cut the number of strokes in half. The stroke goal may be more difficult than the myocardial infarction goal, but it won't happen until we make it happen.

In each case, as we decide to set goals to really improve care outcomes and then figure out the tools needed to achieve each goal, we will quickly see a small number of very important and very practical tools that are reusable for each care improvement agenda.

THE TOOL KITS LOOK A LOT ALIKE

It should not really surprise anyone to learn that for each of the major chronic diseases that currently create 75 percent of health care costs in America, many of the basic tools needed to meet major care improvement goals will look very familiar and very similar — diagnosis, data, care support tools, care protocols, consistent care, and systematic follow-up.

Care reform is very different and lends itself to much more practical planning processes when you start with a real outcome goal and then work backward from the goal to figure out the tools needed to achieve that goal. Tools make a lot more sense when they are clearly needed to achieve some key and strategic aspect of care. Some tools become obvious very quickly when we set our minds to real and consistent care improvement.

EMRS NEED SUPPORT TOOLS

One of the absolutely obvious tools that can make care better for a lot of patients is an electronic medical record (EMR). EMRs make huge sense because when they are well designed and well implemented, they give relevant doctors all the information about all the patients all the time. Real time EMR availability for caregivers in the exam room at the point of care can be a great care asset.

Some people believe that electronic medical records can do most of the heavy lifting on care improvement all by themselves. That, unfortunately, isn't true. EMRs that are not patient focused do not achieve the full potential of the tool. Segmenting electronic records and data storage by either caregiver or by specialty also is a flawed approach. Siloed electronic care information is almost as flawed as siloed paper information. EMRs need to be linked with each other at the patient level — with easy data flow. Even complete electronic medical records can fall short of their full potential if the EMR itself isn't supported by additional computer tools that help doctors sort through the data and point toward desired patterns of care. EMRs need to be part of a total care package, not a stand-alone tool.

PATIENT-FOCUSED EMRS ARE KEY

Benefit packages also need to be thought of as an important tool to support the care process and to help achieve care improvement goals.

Benefit Packages Channel Cash

Benefit packages need to be designed around care goals, not accounting or actuarial issues. Cash is a very powerful influencer of behavior. Cash talks. Think like an economist. Benefit packages channel cash. People tend to overlook that very basic fact of life. Paid benefits *are* real world cash flow for most American providers of care. Cash flow is influential in every business. We need to use the cash flow generated by benefit packages very strategically and skillfully both to encourage desired consumer behavior and to encourage, incent, or disincent specific provider behaviors.

Chapter 5 deals with "the magic of connectors." That chapter explains why getting data flows connected for individual patients is so important for care delivery. We need to use our insurance plan and our government program benefit designs to get patients who need connectors to use connectors — to get care from caregivers who use either care registries or their functional equivalent to support their care. Care registries are an extremely important type and category of connector. We need to use our benefit packages to get patients with certain conditions to use the right connectors, and we need to use benefit design to get caregivers to link with and use effective connectors.

We need every patient with a chronic disease and co-morbidities to have care that is appropriately linked and focused. Chronic care is a team sport, and the caregivers for each patient need to function as a team to achieve optimal care.

That is an incredibly important point to understand. We also need to recognize that someone in the care financing and care delivery process needs to be accountable for the outcomes of the care, and that some entity on the care team needs to have a direct financial impact based on care outcomes. True care reform will not happen until there is a business model that rewards better care. That reward for better care and specific activities does not need to extend to each caregiver involved in the care of every patient. That's actually very hard to do. And not necessary. The reward needs to focus on someone with significant leverage on the care team who can be functionally accountable for the desired care outcomes — a payer or a care team or a health plan or a "medical home" that has both accepted the accountability and has the tools needed to be function-ally accountable.

Accountable care teams equipped with patient data and prepaid for delivering a full package of care are clearly the best and most efficient way of improving care.

WE DON'T NEED TO CHANGE THE ENTIRE PAYMENT SYSTEM

True vertically integrated accountable care teams are not easy to get up. So we need interim solutions. We don't have to change our entire American health care payment system. We need health-plan–like organizations to take on that accountability and then put together the tools and care teams needed to do that work. That new market and care delivery model need to pay for connections, for linkages, for well-coordinated care, and for avoiding medical complications of serious illnesses. Simply getting care-givers connected with each other for each complex patient can make a huge difference in the quality and outcomes of care. We need an entity — like a health plan or a vertically integrated care team — accountable for getting each patient to use connectors and we need relevant caregivers to use connectors. We need to use economic tools and cash flow to make that happen. Fortunately, we have nearly $2.5 trillion in provider revenue that can be channeled to make those behaviors happen.

Again, the magic is to start with the medical goal, figure out how to achieve the goal, figure out what tools are needed to achieve the goal, and then use the payment system to channel provider behavior into those tools and into those care strategies.

DATA IS THE SECRET SAUCE

When we build the strategies to functionally achieve each of those half dozen goals, it becomes very clear very quickly on every single goal that we need real data about care in order to make care better in each goal category. Data-free care will not improve. Data becomes a real tool and a major asset when we have actual care improvement goals in mind. Data can be just a bunch of confusing and even misleading numbers when we don't have any particular goals in mind. Every other industry has already figured that reality out. Factories that successfully do "six sigma" work to build "almost perfect" products use data extensively to achieve their "six sigma" goals. We need to learn from their successes. Those manu-facturers do not collect meaningless, sporadic, intermittent, and random data about their factories, workers, or products. They collect the specific, focused, clearly defined streams of data that are directly relevant to their specific six sigma goals. They focus on their data flow. They collect the exact data they need and they collect that data as they need it.

Again, that is just common sense. The value of data to an industrial six sigma effort is immense, but the data itself only has real value to the busi-ness collecting it because the six sigma production goal can't be achieved without that particular set of data.

HEALTH CARE CAN DO THIS KIND OF WORK

So what can happen when health care providers have a goal and use process engineering or re-engineering and real process data to achieve that goal? Health care achieves the same kind of results that happen in other industries. Costs can drop quality and improve care.

One major health care system in the United States brought the cost of doing heart transplants down by roughly $100,000 per patient. By re-engineering just about every operational aspect of care for those patients, care improved. The reward for the care system was volume — more patients who needed transplants.

In a similar vein, Health Affairs recently published a paper about care teams in India who have completely re-engineered care processes relative to some major types of surgery, and have managed to bring the total costs down for targeted surgeries from $100,000 per case to less than $10,000 per case.[16] Again, the targeted care processes were carefully and extensively re-engineered. The resultant quality of care seems to be consistently high, based on standardized international measurement of surgery outcomes and infection rates, and the cost of care was much lower.

There are no insurance plans in India and very few government programs. So the real world Indian marketplace for care requires a much lower cost "product." Indian hospitals bill the Indian consumers directly for all care. In that context the care business model in India directly encourages and rewards lower prices for packages of care. Low-cost care results from that economic reality.

Health care is not immune from economic incentives or realities. Any time the payment system changes, the care delivery system changes to echo the cash flow change. Any time new goals are set, care delivery can be re-engineered to help achieve those goals.

THREE PROVIDER PAYMENT CHANGES ARE NEEDED

There are three major and obvious areas where changes in payment to providers can be a tool to improve care in America. The first change area is to simply not pay for a select list of "never" events. The second change should relate to chronic care. We need a model that encourages and rewards connections and care teams. The third major change should focus on individual caregiver team performance.

Even though this book is focused on the care improvement opportunities presented by chronic conditions, we should begin the work to set up a market environment where acute care providers can be rewarded for higher quality, better outcomes, and lower prices.

Acute caregivers should ultimately compete in a world where comparative outcomes are relevant and visible to patients. A workable database about relevant care choices and performance could be established over just a few years if both payers and public policy health leaders jointly decide to make it happen. We are beginning to collect important data about a number of areas of hospital performance. That database needs to be expanded and made more "user friendly" so that consumers can make informed choices about hospitals and hospitals can learn where they can focus their care improvement agendas.

WE NEED GOALS

Whether we start exclusively with chronic conditions or choose to throw in a couple of key areas of acute care, the key first step needed to actually improve care is to set goals. We need to set measurable, inspirational, operational, and functional goals that point us clearly and collectively in a given direction. Reducing the number of kidney failures by 50 percent is the kind of goal we need to set. Then we can collectively think through all the things we need to do for future kidney patients to achieve that goal. Reducing asthma crises by 50 percent is also a good goal. Reducing heart attacks and congestive heart failure crises by 50 percent is entirely achievable. Each of those major disease outcome goals can point us to tools and strategies needed to make them real.

Tools result from that process. When we have a goal, tools make sense. Data becomes incredibly relevant. Data collection tools become meaningful investments by caregivers instead of academic exercises for health care bureaucrats.

Health improvement without goals is very likely to fail. Health improvement with goals is much more likely to succeed — particularly if we invest in the tools that the goals require in order to be achieved.

One set of tools that seems to be needed by all the chronic care agendas is a set of "connectors." Connectors are needed in a number of areas to do some very heavy lifting.

The original title for this book was The Magic of Connectors. Why was that the working title? Read on.

Things To Do

4

Connectors Are Magic

The closest thing to real magic for the next generation of health care improvement is "connectors."

We need connectors. Connectors can do wonderful things for the right patients. Nearly 75 percent of all care costs come from patients with chronic conditions. Eighty percent of the care costs for those patients comes from patients with multiple health conditions — co-morbidities. Patients with co-morbidities tend to have separate doctors for each diagnosis because care delivery in America is now very specialized.

As noted earlier, each doctor in each specialty tends to practice in a separate site as a separate business unit, and each doctor tends to keep track of the care they give to each patient on a separate, patient-specific paper medical record.

Each doctor generally stores his or her own paper medical records for the care they personally provided to each patient. The paper medical records are typically sorted and filed in physical file cabinets and the actual cabinets are usually located in each doctor's office.

So a patient with four co-morbidities will usually have four or more separate doctors, with four or more separate paper medical records — and each of the medical records for each patient will be "incomplete" because each record typically only has information about the care delivered in that specific care site by that specific medical business entity to that individual patient for the specific areas and items of care relevant to that office. A few other data elements exist in many of those paper records — usually general medical history and some demographic information that is often self-reported by each patient, but detailed and timely information about actual care delivered by other caregivers usually isn't included in those paper records.

OLDER PATIENTS OFTEN HAVE MAJOR CONNECTION PROBLEMS

Anyone who has tried to help an elderly parent who is very ill with their care knows what a nightmare that whole multiprovider care process can be. It's generally impossible to get a total sense of what care is being delivered — or had been delivered — for each patient. That isn't the doctor's fault. It's a functionality issue. The various doctors usually don't know what the other doctors have done or are doing for each patient because they have no mechanism to communicate that information. So today, far too often, literally no one knows what total set of prescriptions have been written for a single patient or which prescriptions have been actually filled or taken by the patient.

It's a paper-based information jigsaw puzzle with the actual puzzle pieces sitting on separate tables in separate rooms in separate buildings. It is basically "data access chaos," and bad care can result far too often.

Having multiple caregivers is not a rare occurrence for the people with chronic conditions who spend 80 percent of our care dollars. The chart below shows the increased number of medical visits that result when patients have co-morbidities. (See Figure 4.1.)

The current American nonsystem of care clearly does the very worst job of connecting care for the patients with co-morbidities who personally, as patients, need care connectors the most. Those patients are generally

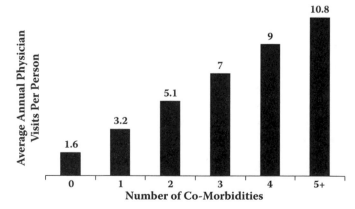

Source: The Silver Book: Chronic Disease and Medical Innovation in an Aging Nation; Partnership for Solutions. Chronic Conditions: Making the case for ongoing care-September 2004 update. Baltimore, MD: Johns Hopkins University. 2004.

Figure 4.1   Physician Visits Increase with Number of Co-Morbidities

on their own when it comes to linking or to connecting care approaches between their various treating physicians.

MEDICAL HOME AND PACKAGES OF CARE

That obvious lack of care coordination in American health care today is why many health reform policy advocates now support increasing the use of several fairly generic care organization concepts like "The Medical Home" or "Primary Care Coordination" for patients with chronic conditions and co-morbidities.

Having a really well-designed and well-organized "medical home" where designated caregivers can coordinate and support all of the care needs of a given patient makes a lot of sense, particularly when a "medical home" is contrasted to uncoordinated, unlinked, unconnected, incident-based patterns of care.

Some reformers who have concerns about fee-based incidents of care are beginning to call for a whole new medical reimbursement model that pays patient-specific teams of caregivers preset amounts of money to take collective care of individual patients with multiple medical conditions. The hope is that if doctors are somehow paid a lump sum per patient as a "team," then team behaviors of some kind will result. That kind of collective payment approach can work very well if the caregivers are already a team and already have economic linkages with one another.

The challenge, of course, is that in order to make that payment model work in the world of pure solo practice caregivers, someone has to first figure out for each patient what the right care team might be and then someone has to figure out how to distribute the prepaid money between the relevant caregivers fairly, equitably, and efficiently. The simple act of distributing pieces of cash among independent and unconnected caregivers is no small challenge. Lining up those teams for each patient is a wee bit difficult to do, particularly since each team, by definition, is patient specific. The act of figuring out exactly who is the relevant caregiver team for a given patient is often not an easy thing to do. In most settings, the functional care teams for different patients will necessarily be different for each patient and each "team" will exist only in the specific and temporary context of each patient. Figuring out workable cash flow mechanisms inside each of those patient-specific teams would not be easy.

Connecting the care of multiple caregivers without any tools or processes to facilitate connectivity makes the job even harder. But the overall goal of creating and rewarding team behaviors is a very good one.

The reality is that if we really do want to cut the number of kidney failures or asthma crises in half, everywhere in America, we need to work today with the current set of disaggregated care entities and provide tools and processes that allow those caregivers to function like a team. The missing link is links. The challenge and the opportunity in working systematically with a world of fiercely independent caregivers to cut the number of kidney failures, heart attacks, or asthma crises in America in half will be to functionally blend their patient care data and medical information, even if we can't actually blend their business entities or their medical practices.

A NEW GENERATION OF CONNECTORS

What we need for all of America's independent doctors and hospitals is another generation of "connectors." If we don't somehow "connect" the care of independent doctors, we will never achieve any of our major care improvement goals. We need to face that stark reality very directly or just give up on achieving any significant goals. We need connectors that create the virtual functionality of team care even when the caregivers are not organized economically, functionally, operationally, or structurally as a team.

CONNECTORS COME IN VARIOUS VERSIONS

American health care is experimenting right now with a wide variety of connector models. Some very wealthy people are opting for "concierge medicine" and, in effect, have decided to hire their own personal care connector to serve as their linkage to the wide world of care. Concierge medicine is, at its core, a kind of connector — just like "medical homes" or designated care coordinators — and can perform various connector functions.

Telephone nurse lines that look at patients' claims files and try to help people find better care strategies and better care practices are also a kind of connector. Some of the new proprietary personal health record systems have services built in that are intended to help patients connect better with their own care. Systems like "Health Vault" are trying, in some very earnest ways, to be rudimentary connectors.

The old HMO primary care "gate keeper" was, in its best versions, a kind of connector. So multiple forms of connectors have their fans and their advocates.

How do other countries deal with that care linkage issue? Most other Western countries have much higher percentages of their physicians in primary care practices and specialties.[1] Most countries work hard to make sure that there are enough primary care doctors to meet their citizens' primary care needs. Primary care doctors, by their very nature, tend to serve as front-level linkages and connectors for patients relative to the larger care system around them. Everyone in Great Britain, for example, has a primary care doctor — "general practitioner" — as a right and privilege of being covered by the National Health Service (NHS). General practitioners (GPs) in Great Britain each have a designated "panel" of patients. The doctor–patient relationship is codified, supported, and enhanced by the existence of those panels. The GPs in Great Britain each focus their personal and professional attention very directly on their own specific panel of patients. That panel structure creates a fairly stable set of doctor–patient relationships. The NHS GPs are functionally care coordinators of sorts, and they serve as a kind of "connector" to care for their patients.

Great Britain is trying to build an electronic medical record (EMR) system to enhance the ability of their primary care infrastructure to improve care. But even without the new electronic support system, the current availability of a primary care doctor for every patient in Great Britain is a huge step in that direction.

We obviously need connectors in the United States. We need our patients with multiple conditions to have mechanisms that link their caregivers and their care.

The easiest to use and most advanced form of connectors that exist now in America are the vertically integrated, multispecialty group practices.

Group practices are in-place care organizations that typically now have many physicians under the same umbrella coordinating care with each other. Care teams inside of multispecialty group practices typically do a fairly good job of coordinating care with each other because they are usually structured in part to do exactly that. Most of those multispecialty care settings begin with and nurture a culture of collaborative care. The Mayo Clinic, Cleveland Clinic, Health Partners Clinics, Geisinger Clinic, Group Health Clinics, Intermountain Healthcare, and The Permanente Medical Groups all use that model of having physicians from multiple specialties working together and connected to each other in the context of one shared practice.

The physicians in each multispecialty group also are highly likely to be sharing a single melded medical record and working together to some degree to coordinate patient care. Not surprisingly, multispecialty group practices have moved far more quickly than the rest of American health care to adopt and implement EMRs. It's actually hard to find a major multispecialty medical group that does not have some form of EMR.

Vertical integration has its own obvious care coordination advantages — with information inside those large caregiver teams flowing more smoothly from the medical offices to the hospital settings and back again to each physician who cares for each patient.

VIRTUAL INTEGRATION CAN MIMIC VERTICAL INTEGRATION

Vertical integration is a lovely model. It's also relatively rare in America. Most caregivers are neither vertically nor horizontally integrated. So what can we do for care settings that aren't vertically integrated? We can use computers to help facilitate coordination. We can create "virtual" integration.

It's becoming increasingly possible to use well-designed computer systems to bring other sets of otherwise separate caregivers together into functioning care teams that can be "virtually" integrated to a large degree for the care of individual patients.

It's a much better option than no linkages at all. It's a lot easier to link solo caregivers by computer than it is to get them to give up their life-long commitment to economic independence and become full business partners with other doctors for every single functional and economic thing that they do.

EMR PLUS CARE SUPPORT TOOLS

It is amazing how effective care can be when it is both coordinated and consistently delivered. A couple of pilot "connection" programs have shown that to be true.

Denver Improved Outcomes

Kaiser Permanente has recently computerized the medical records of about 10 million people. The caregivers at Kaiser Permanente are now learning how to use that new array of data. Pilots are being run in multiple settings to figure out how to optimize use of the new array of data that is now sitting in the Kaiser Permanente EMR. It is becoming very clear that the EMR data is most useful when it is coordinated with a care connection support tool. For the Kaiser Permanente medical team in Denver, for example, a system was set up to extract data from the EMR relative to each patient who had a diagnosis of either coronary artery disease or congestive heart failure.

A "care registry" was developed to support care for that particular target set of chronic care patients. The registry pulled data from the Kaiser Permanente EMR and linked each patient's primary care doctors, cardiologists, pharmacists, and nurses. The computerized portion of the system very consistently reminded every caregiver what care was needed for each heart patient at each point of contact.

The system also scanned the EMR for each patient constantly to see if tests were needed or if patient prescriptions had been filled or refilled. The system triggered targeted follow-up and outreach. The care team of doctors, nurses, and pharmacists, for example, helped patients who didn't refill their prescriptions — often based on various side effects — find other drugs or therapies that met the same medical need for the patient but generated fewer complications or concerns for individual patients.

The Death Rate Dropped

The results were extremely encouraging. The heart care delivered to those patients in Colorado had already been at or above community standards before the new registry system was developed and implemented. The new care-registry-supported approach created even better care, cutting the total death rate for those two major heart conditions for those registry-supported patients by 72 percent in just a couple of years.[2]

Every single heart patient was in the pilot. That very high success level wasn't based on a medically nonrepresentative subset of the target population.

The connector worked. That success did not happen because of brand new "science" or theories about heart care. The doctors and nurses and pharmacists on that Kaiser Permanente Colorado care team all knew what the right thing to do was for each patient before the new support system was put in place. The missing link for the caregivers in Colorado wasn't pure or new medical knowledge. It was reminders, triggers, prompts. Medical blocking and tackling. It was a new tool that created electronic supported care follow-through — absolute consistency — supported by real-time patient-specific information.

Triple Co-Morbidities in Hawaii

Care registries can be very useful connectors. In a similar pilot in Hawaii, the local care team took every Kaiser Permanente patient who had all three of the major chronic diseases — diabetes, coronary artery disease, and congestive heart failure — and did a similar computer-supported team care approach. Keep in mind that patients who have all three of those chronic conditions are people who need a lot of care support. They are also people who often, in America, have their care very badly linked because they generally have separate sets of caregivers and care sites.

In Hawaii, those patients already had a team of caregivers. The computer-supported care project gave their caregivers a new tool to use to improve care. Two tools were used: the new EMR and the new "panel support tool."

In Hawaii, the medical record identified the target group of patients. The care protocols for those patients were embedded in the "panel support tool." That combination of support tools helped the caregivers manage their patients' care with a very high level of proactive consistency.

What happened? The result for those triple co-morbidity patients was very similar to the Colorado results. The number of hospital admissions needed for those very sick registry-supported patients dropped by over 60 percent in six months, and the number of emergency room visits for those same patients dropped by nearly one third.

PREVENTING ER VISITS IS A VERY GOOD THING TO DO

Care support tools work. The magic is to connect the caregivers, connect the data, and create consistent care. Those packages of computer tools have been proven to work in multiple settings — not just vertically integrated care teams who have an EMR. Quite a few community clinics in the United States have been developing their own versions of care registries to help support care for their patients. Denver Health has been a leader in that area. The New York City public hospital system has done some important and successful pioneering work in those areas. The need for hospitalizations for chronic care patients has dropped significantly in both settings.

CARE REGISTRY WORKED FOR "SAFETY NET" PATIENTS

In one non-Kaiser care setting involving a network of safety net clinics who are primarily focused on both Medicaid patients and the local totally uninsured population, a very similar care registry was set up to support care for heart patients and for diabetic patients with co-morbidities.[3] In that non-Kaiser community care setting, many of the doctors rotated shifts. Some were volunteers. Some were students. The patients who came to the clinics and then returned to the same clinics for care often saw entirely new caregivers on quite a few visits, so continuity of care in those clinics functionally could not come exclusively from the traditional doctor–patient personal relationship. The new care registry that was implemented in those clinics filled that gap and created a continuity of care that very consistently "connected the caregivers" for each patient.

The registry in those clinics kept track of all care and reminded the current caregiver who happened to be on duty when patients come in for care exactly what care, tests, or therapies each registry-supported patient needed at that moment.

Hospital Admissions Were Reduced by 70 Percent

That program was also spectacularly successful. It cut the needed hospital admissions for those very low income and high need patients by more than 70 percent.

A sad consequence of that success level in reducing hospital usage was that the program (and the registry support process) was almost killed. Why? Because the safety net hospital that supported the community clinics needed all of the hospital admissions from all of the insured patients to support its hospital and make its payroll solvent. So the hospital sadly decided it might need to kill the care registry.

The physicians who ran the community clinics in that setting appealed that decision and ultimately renegotiated a compromise solution. They agreed not to use the registry for any patients with Medicaid coverage or for any patients with private insurance coverage. They used it only for their patients who were entirely uninsured. That compromise was accepted and the registry continued to function — but it was used exclusively for completely uninsured patients.

Why could the hospital afford to allow completely uninsured patients to use the registry? Think like an economist. The safety net hospital clearly did not have a financial problem if completely uninsured patients were not admitted to the hospital for care. That, in fact, was actually a financial benefit because it reduced costs for the hospital from those safety net patients who generated no revenue at all. The hospital only needed to protect — and continue — the admissions for the patients who paid for their care.

So the irony was that the very best care in that care infrastructure — computer supported, extremely consistent, highly focused, registry-based care — was given only to people with no insurance at all. And the admission rates for patients with chronic conditions went up roughly 70 percent if you had insurance of any kind.

Chapter 1 of this book talked about the sad and unintended consequences that can sometimes result from this country's currently often perverse payment approaches. That strategic rationing of registry use in that particular care environment to not serve paying patients and only alleviate the inpatient care needs of nonpaying patients is a great example of absolutely unintended and perverse consequences for American care delivery and financing.

WE NEED TO CONNECT EVERYONE
WHO NEEDS TO BE CONNECTED

So what do we need to do in America relative to connectors and care registries? We need to connect everyone who needs to be connected. We need computerized care support tools to keep track of certain patients and remind both them and their doctors of what care is currently needed.

Ten percent of our patients use 80 percent of our care dollars. More than 80 percent of those care dollars are spent on patients with co-morbidities and multiple caregivers. We need to track and coordinate care for those patients and caregivers.

If we continue to try to deliver care through uncoordinated, unlinked, and unconnected caregivers, we will not be able to significantly improve care. If we can't ultimately improve care, we will end up having to ration it. That's not a good plan.

We need benefit plans that move patients with co-morbidities into much better connected care. We also need real goals to reduce kidney failures by 50 percent, so that registries are a tool that will be actually used by caregivers to improve care, and so we know collectively what tools we need and what we are trying to do with each tool.

BUYERS NEED TO CHANGE THE CASH FLOW

Changing the focus of care improvement to targeted chronic care conditions will not happen until some elements of the cash flow for health care change. Money needs to be spent on creating team care for chronic patients, and money needs to be spent to get chronic care patients with co-morbidities into care supported by registries and care plans.

So who can change the cash flow to make that happen? Buyers. Only purchasers can make that cash flow change happen. Large employers who buy health coverage for their employees could and should lead the way to support a better approach to care. Government agencies should follow as soon as the new models show how well they work.

Buyers need to make a few key decisions at this point if we really want to improve care. Buyers have a huge and critical role to play at this stage of health care reform, because only buyers have the ability to change the way key aspects of care are purchased. Large employers already use detailed, well-designed purchasing specifications for all the other goods and services that they purchase. Extending purchasing expertise to health care is a logical next step when Starbucks is spending more money on health care than they do on coffee[4] — and General Motors spends more on health care than they do on steel.[5]

BUYERS SHOULD SPECIFY THE CONTEXT FOR CARE

How can buyers change the way health care is delivered? Buyers could choose to select only caregivers and health plans that use connected care. Or buyers could give consumers choices between connected and unconnected caregivers, but could require employees who use unconnected care to pay more. The health insurance market is very competitive. Health plans want to keep customers and gain customers. Employers have a lot of very real leverage with their health plans — leverage that buyers often underutilize. Buyers could simply require their insurers and health plans to use some combination of benefit designs and educational tools to steer appropriate patients to appropriate connectors and appropriate caregivers.

Buyers can write those steerage and functionality requirements into their purchasing specifications and then simply ask each health plan or benefits administrator to perform.

THE POINT OF CONNECTORS IS TO CONNECT

There are several "connector" options that buyers can support. Some creativity is very likely at this point. The point of the whole connector agenda is the actual connection function. It's not to use a specific tool.

Several options can work very well. What should not be an option for the next generation of American health care is to allow totally unconnected care, and buyers who select health plans should simply require their plans to support the use of connectors for the patients with co-morbidities.

In the best of all possible worlds, connectors would be functioning for caregivers and patients in a world of fully computerized care databases. If every care site in America had a linkable EMR, modern computer technology is already clearly capable of linking all those computer systems into a registry database for the 5 to 10 percent of the population who most need the support of care connectors.

That world of full EMR-linked connectivity will not happen quickly except for a few multispecialty group practice care sites, but we need connectors for our most complex patients now. What can we do about that? We clearly need an interim electronic database to feed the new care connectors.

CLAIMS DATA CAN BE USED

There is a database that can be used more quickly for that purpose. That database is the one built and run by payers. It contains the payer-based claims-triggered information that care providers in America already send to payers about the diagnosis, procedures, caregivers, and care delivered to individual patients. That care data is relatively comprehensive, constantly maintained, based on common procedure and diagnosis codes, and consistent in its use of provider identification codes. It isn't used very often to support care delivery, but it could be. The data isn't as comprehensive or as timely as an EMR, but a claims database can definitely work to trigger and support care registries for the five percent of our patients who most need linked care. A full-boat interconnected EMR clearly has the best data, but until we have EMRs more widely in place — in the interim — the currently available claims data is probably our best hope for short-term care improvement, using various versions of care registries as a form of mini-EMR for targeted populations.

The next chapter deals with care connections within the context of completely computerized care support. Creating highly effective connectors can be done most easily inside "the perfect system." As we computerize growing aspects of health care, we should understand clearly why we are doing that work, what we want to accomplish, and we should have a collective sense of what "the perfect system" should look like when we are done.

Computerization will inevitably permeate health care. Our recovery package for the country will be funding electronic support for care. As we bring computers into various aspects of care, we are more likely to get an optimal benefit from those computers if we start with a clear goal for where we should end up. What do we want computers in health care to do for us? That's the next chapter of this book.

5

The Perfect System

Health care needs and deserves the perfect computer system. We should begin with that goal and build our national and collective system agenda and IT investment strategy with the creation of a perfect system as our clearly targeted end point.

What would a perfect system for health care look like? We need to be very clear from the beginning what our expectations for a perfect system are if we are going to invest billions of dollars in health care IT as part of the national economic recovery agenda. We should be very focused on building the essence of the right system. We don't want to lay that track twice.

ALL, ALL, AND THEN ALL

The perfect system for care should have "all of the information about all of the patients all of the time." Real time care data. Comprehensive care data. Data for everyone. All, all, and all.

That single very basic goal should define, direct, channel, guide, and inform our overall American health care system's agenda.

It would be breathtakingly stupid to put health care data on the computer and end up with the same sets of isolated, inaccessible, noninteractive information silos we have now with paper medical records. We need all the information about each patient. We need that information all the time — whenever and wherever care is being delivered.

Caregivers should not have to guess about their patient's prior diagnosis or treatments. Caregivers should not be ignorant of patient medications or relevant test results. Caregivers for each patient should know all of the medical information about each patient, and caregivers should have that information available in real time at the point of care. That should be our goal. We should settle for nothing less.

Medicine is an information dependent science that operates far too often with a highly dysfunctional information deficit. That is wrong. We need to do better.

INFORMATION SECURITY IS ESSENTIAL

If we really want optimal care, we need optimal information. Information security needs to be an absolute expectation as part of the package. That almost goes without saying. But it needs to be said.

Personal care information needs to be personal. We need real time and complete information to provide care and to track care and to do world class research about care. We need that information to be appropriately confidential so that it is used exclusively to support health and care.

Anyone who violates patient confidentiality and violates that confidentiality for some form of monetary gain, personal coercion, or to damage the reputation or credibility of a patient should be treated and penalized as a criminal. We need strict standards on use of data and we need strict penalties for people who willfully misuse data.

CQI IS NEEDED — AND CQI NEEDS DATA

We very much need data. Care coordination cannot happen without data. Continuous care improvement simply cannot happen without data. No industry has ever done continuous improvement without data. Optimal medical research cannot happen without data.

The really good news is that we are on the cusp of a golden age for medical research. Most medical research done in the world today involves very small numbers of patients. The research is done most often to justify the sale of a drug or a product. When the "justification" process that triggered the research has achieved its goal of getting the product to market, the research about the effect of that product usually ends. So we often don't know what the long-term impact of a product or pharmaceutical is for patients in any systematic way.

That is a really bad information deficit. Why does it exist? Think like an economist. Follow-up doesn't happen for the majority of those research projects today because there is no business model that rewards follow-up.

If anything, follow-up research might run the "business" risk of the manufacturer learning that a profitable product might be dangerous or dysfunctional over time. The people who own the product and fund the research don't necessarily want to learn that their product is more problematic over time. So they often don't build follow-up research into their budgets.

Follow-up research also doesn't happen because the information pieces needed to actually do adequate follow-up research on most new products, devices, technologies, drugs, or treatment approaches are almost always entirely patient specific. Therefore, the information about any product is scattered into thousands and even millions of unconnected, isolated, hard-to-decipher paper medical records with no way of pulling out the needed information other than to have individual, on-site researchers manually find, pull, and read each and every individual patient's paper chart to look for information relevant to the product or treatment. Ouch.

That's an embarrassingly inadequate situation. As we look at building the "perfect system" for health care, we should not accept that situation any longer. The health care community should know year by year the ongoing success rate or failure rate of each kind of implant and each kind of treatment for each kind of patient, and should be able to use that information to make future decisions about care — both for new patients and for the patients who already have the implant or the prescription or the type of care.

That level of specific treatment follow-up can be invaluable. A few recent successes in those areas give us a sense of what is possible. Kaiser Permanente has already used its own computerized database to track the long-term impact of people using VIOXX for pain relief and discovered serious downstream outcomes for a number of patients.[1] VIOXX ultimately was removed from the market. Kaiser Permanente also used its current database to look at the longer-term outcome for patients with various types of heart stents. That research uncovered some concerns about patient outcomes over longer periods of time relative to some stents. The caregivers involved in that research ultimately recommended that patients with some stents be put on lifetime follow-up medication to reduce the risk of future heart damage. The manufacturers were not doing that research. Likewise, follow-up research into the Kaiser Permanente computerized registry of joint replacements showed major differences in the outcomes for different care approaches.

AMERICAN HEALTH CARE NEEDS A CULTURE OF CONTINUOUS LEARNING

That kind of follow-up research should be standard for every aspect of health care. It cannot happen and will not happen until we have data and the data is available for research.

Remember the basic and fundamental goal we need for The Perfect System in America: All, All, and then All.

When all of the data is available for all of the patients, longitudinal tracking of the long-term impacts of a given drug or implant or surgical procedure will become the basic working knowledge base for care, rather than a rare event, done infrequently, shared inconsistently, and seldom replicated.

So why is the recommendation for The Perfect System the goal that caregivers should have all of the information about all of the patients all of the time and why have caregivers at Kaiser Permanente adopted that basic data availability standard as a goal? It's helpful to understand that Kaiser Permanente has gone through a relatively useful learning curve over the past couple of years about the use of computer systems to improve care. This is probably a good time to share some of that learning.

MOST OF HEALTH CARE IS SPLINTERED

This is not a book about Kaiser Permanente. But to understand the nature of the multi-year Kaiser Permanente learning process about computer support for care, it's probably useful to get a quick sense of how Kaiser Permanente is structured and how Kaiser Permanente has begun to use computers. The current investment in computer support at Kaiser Permanente is slightly over $4 billion, so there has been a recent chance to do some serious learning.

As noted earlier in this book, most of American health care is divided into separate, unlinked, unconnected pieces — independent business units that often compete with each other for patients and market share. Hospitals compete with other hospitals. Within a given hospital, there can be anywhere from a couple of separate physician practices to hundreds of separate physician practices. A given hospital might have several sets of surgeons, several sets of oncologists, multiple independent internists, a raft of unlinked family practitioners, and a whole array of independent pediatricians, obstetricians, and various medical specialists and subspecialists. They usually all compete with each other for patients.

There are a lot of competitors in care delivery. Pharmacists compete with other pharmacists. Drug stores compete with drug stores. Labs compete with labs. And all that vast array of competing independent caregivers tends to get paid by another array of competing health plans, insurance companies, and various government program payers, like Medicare, Medicaid, the Veterans Administration, and some local welfare programs.

It's an uneasy set of relationships most of the time. Most of the providers complain about most of the health plans relatively often, and most of the health plans have an arm's length and sometimes problematic relationship with most of the caregivers. There are exceptions, but that is a fairly common set of realities.

The net result of that morass of competing and siloed business entities is that cooperation levels are often amazingly low. Getting each of the independent surgeons and surgical groups at a given hospital to simply agree on the best surgical tray to use for patients in that hospital can be an almost insurmountable task.

Agreeing on a common computer database is even more unlikely. Health care in America is splintered into an amazingly complex set of silos and pieces and separate, independent business units, and each business entity tends to have its own separate data filing system.

So how is Kaiser Permanente different from that normal care delivery context, and why does that difference cause Kaiser Permanente to think differently in some key ways about how computers can and should support care? Kaiser Permanente is a vertically integrated care system that has embedded — inside its own functional umbrella structure — all the key elements of care. Kaiser Permanente is basically a caregiver. Hospitals, clinics, pharmacies, laboratories, imaging centers, home health programs, health educators, and multiple other types of care are included inside Kaiser Permanente as part of a "vertically integrated" care model.

Kaiser Permanente serves about 8.5 million people with a staff of about 160,000 employees and nearly 600 care sites. The Permanente Medical Groups may be the largest private medical groups in the world. The Permanente physicians exclusively treat Kaiser Permanente patients. So Kaiser Permanente is basically a very "vertical" provider of care.

Kaiser Permanente also is a health plan. As a health plan, Kaiser Permanente enrolls the members who became the Kaiser Permanente care system patients. In its entirety, Kaiser Permanente is an almost self-contained blended model of financing and care delivery.

The total Kaiser Permanente organization serves a population bigger than 40 states and 140 countries,[2] and currently has an annual revenue flow of $40 billion.[3] The Kaiser Permanente infrastructure is big enough to create and sustain its own health care eco-system and data flow capabilities.

So Kaiser Permanente thinks a bit differently and more comprehensively and holistically about linkages, support systems, and shared data flow than most elements of U.S. care delivery. Kaiser Permanente can and does think about computer systems and data flow from the perspective of comprehensive patient care, rather than the perspective of competitive patient care.

Kaiser Permanente set a goal several years ago to implement care-focused computer systems that would give all the doctors all the information about all the patients all the time. As noted above, Kaiser Permanente has invested roughly $4 billion to do that work and achieve that goal. The Kaiser Permanente HealthConnect electronic medical record (EMR) project is probably the biggest single private systems project ever done in any industry anywhere in the world. It has been successful, and every Kaiser Permanente Medical Group physician now exclusively uses the Kaiser Permanente HealthConnect medical record for his or her patient care. Every single Kaiser Permanente patient now has an electronic record instead of a paper record.

Paper medical record systems for Kaiser Permanente clinics disappeared between 2004 and 2008.

ONE-THIRD REDUCTION IN BROKEN BONES

As a result of having that new database, Kaiser Permanente is engaged in a number of processes and programs to improve care. No one has ever had all that electronic information about patients before, so there is a major learning process underway. The Hawaii and Denver projects mentioned in Chapter 4 that made major improvements in care for chronic care patients in their geographic areas have been and are part of that overall learning process. A similar computer system–supported "Healthy Bones" program that was set up two years ago for all seniors in Southern California has managed to cut the number of hip fractures for those patients by 37 percent.[4] The EMR was used to help the Southern California care teams focus on the needs of seniors at risk of bone damage. The whole effort was extremely successful. Healthy Bones programs are now rolling out to all Kaiser Permanente care sites.

If a similar Healthy Bones program could ultimately be implemented for the entire country, that effort could reduce broken bones for all American patients by over 100,000 bones a year.[5] That's a lot of people who could be walking instead of limping, being pushed in a wheelchair, or functionally immobile.

Other care sites in America make more money when bones break, so those kinds of prevention programs don't exist now in most care settings in America.

So what do these successes tell us as a country in need of health reform? Because Kaiser Permanente is a total care system and basically plays every position on the health care field, Kaiser Permanente naturally thinks of systems from the perspective of the total patient, not just as a specialty-defined or care-site-defined piece of the patient. So Kaiser Permanente has had very good operational and functional reasons to figure out what an optimal data flow should look like for health care.

The question that was defined years ago by the medical brain trust at Kaiser Permanente was, "How can we use computer systems to help improve care?" The answer to that question was to build computer systems that are focused on patients, not on care sites or caregivers, and to create complete information connectivity, not electronic data silos.

"All, All and then All" was the first goal. The second goal created for the care support computer systems was equally clear: "Make the right thing easy to do."

MAKE THE RIGHT THING EASY TO DO

That may seem like more of a slogan than a strategic agenda, but when you begin to think systematically about care improvement, the importance of both elements of that goal become clear. We, as a national care infrastructure, need to figure out the "right thing" and then we need to "make it easy to do." That goal is so simple it is profound. It's a great guide for system design.

Why are those two goals and that learning relevant to the rest of American health care? Because computers are obviously and inevitably going to be used by all American caregivers — fairly soon. Decisions made now about system design, content, and desired use will affect how well that ultimate macro system of electronic data functions for all Americans in the future.

We, as a country, should not allow system development for health care to simply develop haphazardly or grow in silos. Thinking of computer support solely in the context of single care sites, single specialties, or single testing processes will never get us to optimal care results. We are starting in a deep hole as a country.

As noted repeatedly in this book, health care does not currently have a robust data support infrastructure in this country. That infrastructure will, however, be built in some form or another over the next few years because lots of people are now trying to computerize individual pieces of care. It would be very possible to build that ultimate infrastructure entirely wrong. It would have been incredibly stupid for Kaiser Permanente, for example, to build one computerized database for surgeons and another, unlinked and unrelated, computerized database for internists. Having stand-alone and unconnected data silos for allergists and neurologists would have been a very bad strategy for Kaiser Permanente to follow. Not having all pharmaceutical information available in each patient's database would also have been both silly and dangerous.

THE PATIENT SHOULD BE THE FOCUS OF CARE DATA

The key has to be to have the patient be the focus of the data pool — not the care provider — and to figure out the specific connectors needed to bring together all the care data for each patient who needs their care connected.

Connectors are critically important. As stated in Chapter 4, we can't really cut kidney failures in half as a country unless the full team of doctors working with each high-risk kidney patient is working in synch to make care better for those patients.

TEN CRITERIA FOR ULTIMATE SYSTEM DESIGN

So in a nutshell, the Kaiser Permanente learning about data systemness is that the new American health care database should be

1. Patient focused
2. Complete
3. Accessible by all relevant parties
4. Current (real time, if possible)
5. Easy to use
6. Linked to care improvement programs
7. Accessible to patients as well as caregivers
8. Transportable (when people change health plans or caregivers)
9. Interoperable
10. Confidential — with confidentiality enforced

How is that general strategy working so far for Kaiser Permanente patients?

SIX MILLION E-VISITS

It is a work in progress — and progress is being made. Kaiser Permanente patients now all have secure access at home to their own medical records.

Patients can also do e-scheduling, get lab results electronically, and have e-visits and hold secure messaging e-dialogues with their own Kaiser Permanente doctor. Last year, in California alone, Kaiser Permanente patients had over six million e-visits with their physicians. Most of those visits were in lieu of the patient having to drive to a clinic, check in, wait in a waiting room, wait in an exam room, talk to the doctor, get dressed, check out, and then drive back to work or home. Instead, three million times, the patient simply put the relevant question on the computer and pushed "send."

Secure messaging and e-visits done by physicians with a high level of medical confidence are possible today because each Kaiser Permanente doctor receiving the electronic message from their patient can now instantly pop up that patient's complete care data on their own screen to be fully informed about all the patient's current care-related medical history before sending back a response.

That kind of connectivity and informed interaction between patients and caregivers is a path that will make sense ultimately for all of American health care. It won't happen to any scale, in most settings, however, until physicians receiving the e-mail from their patients have convenient electronic access to that patient's medical records or — minimally — to the patient's electronic personal health records (PHRs).

Connecting data from multiple care sites and caregivers should be a top priority goal for the future of computerization in American health care.

ALL NEW SYSTEMS SHOULD BE CONNECTABLE

Any new hospital or private practice computer system implemented from this date forward should be set up to have the ability to connect data electronically with both payers and other caregivers. Both buyers and payers have the potential to play a major role fairly quickly in facilitating health care data connectivity. The current claims-based electronic care data sitting in the payer computers should be made available in a standardized format to both patients and caregivers. Right now — in a typical, American highly splintered care environment — a given patient might see six doctors and use two or more separate, unlinked hospitals. A recent Medicare analysis of patients with multiple co-morbidities showed that the patients saw an average of more than a dozen doctors each in the prior two years. None of those care sites usually has any way of knowing about the actual care delivered at the other care sites. Most caregivers in America today have no transportable data except for pieces of paper. And that data is not connected with any other health care data in any useful way.

THE PERFECT SYSTEM IS POSSIBLE

So what should the perfect system look like? Complete connectivity should be the goal. Lab tests, electronic images, and diagnostic tool outputs should all flow electronically to the care site of the relevant doctor for each patient.

EMRs and labs should exchange data electronically, not using a data flow involving intermittent chunks of paper output that is subsequently re-entered — usually manually — into someone's computer system to achieve electronic storage status.

Patients should ultimately have complete connectivity in their homes. Telemedicine is already a good tool for certain conditions. Electronic monitoring of high-need patients can be done from the home. Pilot programs in various sites are doing that now. Mechanisms that track blood sugar levels, weight, physical activity or inactivity, and even mental functioning can all be installed now in homes and linked electronically, in real time, to appropriate caregivers and care teams. Video medicine should definitely be part of the next round of care connectors.

Eliminating many doctors' office visits should be a clearly defined goal of care support system design. Eliminating a major percentage of emergency room visits ought to be another system goal.

Cell phones can, should, and will become more versatile care connections both for the spoken word and for lab results and care instructions. The creativity levels will exceed anything we can think of now. One new system being piloted uses the cell phone to photograph every single food item that the patient eats each day and computes both likely calorie counts and the possible health impacts of the photographed food. The use of cell phones to transform pieces of care is going to quickly go past care delivery enhancements that we thought were possible just a few years ago.

People who advocate for The Medical Home should think of that concept from two perspectives: (1) creating a medical site that is the coordinating home for a given patient's care, and (2) the actual home, itself, with each patient's place of residence connected electronically in appropriate ways with each patient's caregivers.

Ultimately, systems should become a fully embedded tool of caregivers and care. That process is just getting underway.

In the interim, some caregivers like Kaiser Permanente, The Mayo Clinic, Health Partners, The Geisinger Clinics, and The Cleveland Clinic already have EMRs for their patients. Some are beginning to extend the linkages into the patient's workplace and home. Patients at those multispecialty clinics can now get electronic access to their own medical information. In some settings e-visits, e-scheduling, e-consults, and e-supported behavior change models are all already in full operational status.

PERSONAL HEALTH RECORDS
CAN FILL PART OF THE GAP

Patients who don't have a full level of complete EMR-based data available from their caregiver should and could be able relatively soon to get an interim level of connectivity with fairly complete care data through payer-based standardized Internet-available PHRs from their health plans. As noted earlier, that claims database is now badly underused for care improvement and it can be the basis for computerized, Internet-accessible PHR functionality.

Buyers should demand that their payers produce at least PHRs for their employees. Most American health plans — if required to do so — can already produce some type of PHRs for their enrollees. Most patients with direct electronic access to their own computerized PHR report a high level of satisfaction with that access.[6] The PHR can be a very useful care support tool and it should be both encouraged and required by all payers.

It should also be relatively easy to link data from the claims flow and the PHRs to appropriately designated registry databases for each patient, particularly if the payers require the PHRs be designed to achieve that goal.

It will be fairly easy for well-motivated health plans to designate a service or a caregiver to monitor the care delivered in each registry, to be sure that appropriate care is being delivered for each patient.

The logistical challenge that needs to be solved in most settings will be to get the relevant data from the registry to each relevant doctor at the actual point, time, and site of care. Ideally, the various health plan system teams should set up a shared linkage into the registry databases so all providers can connect to the Internet and get linked to the care registries designated by the buyers for their patients. That level of single contact entry point is being piloted now by multiple health plans and caregivers for real-time claims input and adjudication. A similar linkage is a very good idea for registry functionality.

HUB AND SPOKE CONNECTIVITY CAN BE COMPUTER SUPPORTED

Ultimately, electronic care connectivity could transform care in America and across the planet. Computer technology and connectivity can transform care everywhere. It's not hard to imagine a fully computerized hub-and-spoke level of connectivity for third world countries (and even medically underserved rural America).

VIRTUAL CARE IN REMOTE SITES

Telemedicine has a great future. It can bring high levels of expertise very efficiently and effectively to the exact sites where the care is needed.

Solid telemedicine linkages are not very far into our own future. Pilots are being done in various American sites now. In some cases, the care is being linked into people's homes; in other cases, the information links go to remote American care sites staffed by front-level care support people. Those same kinds of tiered, computer-supported knowledge and care linkages may be the key to the only possible care design model that might work logistically for much of rural Africa, India, and China.

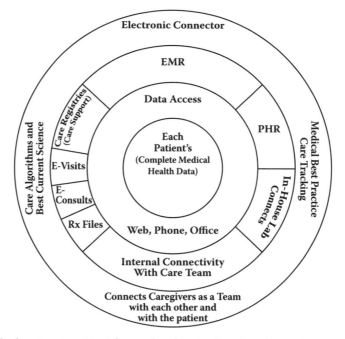

The ideal system is patient focused and patient centered — and uses the computer to record, report, link, and support the delivery of care

Figure 5.1   Support Systems Needed — Patient-Centered Systems

NEXT STEP — CONNECTIVITY

Right now, in this country, we need to computerize care. We need to connect care. We need to connect caregivers.

We need data to track care outcomes and to continuously improve care. We need data for ongoing medical research. We need patients to know what works and we need caregivers to know what works.

We also need to make the right thing easy to do. It might be a good idea to take advantage of the learning cycle that Kaiser Permanente had been on relative to using computers to help support care and use the 10 criteria for ultimate system design outlined earlier as a framework for making strategic decisions about IT investments for the country.

If we start with the premise that we need all the information about all the patients all the time, then we can develop various system elements in various places — and the linkages will be there. It's a little like the Internet — creating a web of interactive data flow — rather than silos of unconnected

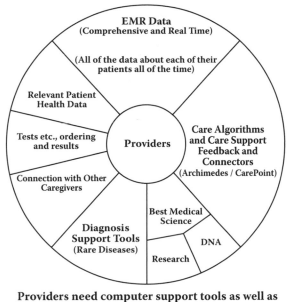

**Providers need computer support tools as well as
all of the data real time for each patient.**

Figure 5.2   Support Systems Needed — Provider-Centered Systems

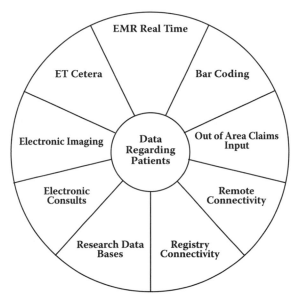

The database, itself, should be real time and paper free.

Figure 5.3   Support Systems Needed — Data Base/Data Flow-Centered Support Systems

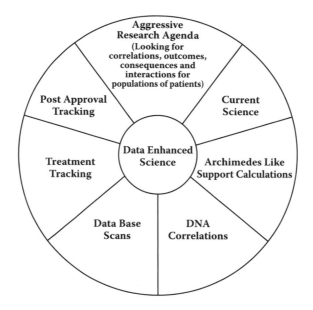

Research can be enhanced immeasurably with the availability of a comprehensive real time database, DNA data, other research data, and patient status.

Figure 5.4   Support Systems Needed — Science Support for Culture of Continuous Learning

health care data locked into separate machines. We simply need better data about care and we need it whenever caregivers deliver care.

We spend $2.5 trillion on care in this country. We should keep track of the care we deliver and we should make our care better. To do that really well, we need everyone to have health coverage. We need everyone in the database. We need everyone in the database on The Perfect System.

Covering everyone is the right next step. Let's look at why that is true.

6

We Need Universal Coverage, Care System Reform, and Care System Competition

The United States is the only industrialized country in the world that does not have universal health care coverage for its citizens.

That fact should be an embarrassment and shame to us all. We spend nearly $2.5 trillion on care and we spend nearly 50 percent more of our Gross National Product (GNP) on health care than the rest of the industrialized world.[1] Yet we have over 46 million completely uninsured people and at least 10 million more seriously underinsured people.[2]

We can't blame our inability to cover everyone on a reluctance on the part of Americans to use the Canadian single payer system for our health coverage. That's the wrong way to look at the universal coverage issue. Every other industrialized country covers all of their citizens and not one uses the Canadian model. The Canadian single payer system exists only in Canada.

Other countries use a variety of paths to cover everyone. Some countries use both multiple health plans and private care providers. On one end of the continuum, a few Scandinavian countries have the government own the entire care system and directly employ the care providers. Most others use a mixed model of government care and private care. Some European countries completely exclude the government from the entire process. Those countries use only private caregivers and they provide all coverage to their people exclusively through competing private, completely nongovernment health insurers — with no government coverage at all. The only thing we can conclude from looking at each of the many countries who have achieved universal coverage is that no two countries have chosen the same model. The models vary significantly from country to country. What does not vary is that every European country and some non-European countries have managed to cover all of their citizens. And we have not.

Chapter 7 deals with various issues about risk pools and health screens that are now used in U.S. health insurance and suggests ways we can make those screens disappear in America. This chapter is intended to make two simple and basic points. One point is that we should modify the model we use to create competition and better performance in health care. The second point is that we need to meld universal coverage with care improvement as a single blended agenda. If we really want to reform and significantly improve health care delivery in America, we need to have health care coverage for everyone in America. We need everyone covered so we can improve everyone's care. And we need a market model that allows people to make informed choices about care delivery options, care-givers, and teams of caregivers.

INTERMITTENT COVERAGE DISRUPTS CARE

Why do we need universal coverage to reform care? We can't reform care for patients with asthma if the patients have insurance part of the time and don't have insurance part of the time. We can't track care for asthma patients if we don't have the information to tell us what care is being deliv-ered to asthma patients. We need a longitudinal database on each child who has asthma so that we can cut the number of asthma crises in half — and we need to collectively recognize the truth that the only practical way of having longitudinal care data on each child is to also have longitudinal coverage data on each child.

Coverage continuity creates data continuity. We need data to fix care. We need everyone in the database, at the level where data helps improve care.

Universal coverage is needed to fix care. To repeat a key point — If we want to reduce the number of crisis-level asthma attacks for American kids by 50 percent we need to cover 100 percent of the kids. All of the time.

The same reality is true for patients with diabetes and patients with heart failure. We can make major improvements in care delivery if we have a longitudinal database on each person suffering from those diseases. We can't systematically improve care for people who fall in and out of the system and who fall in and out of the database. Simply having patients slipping in and out of the database obviously makes systematic care improvement much more difficult.

CARE IMPROVEMENT NEEDS COVERAGE CONTINUITY

Care improvement should be a universal American health policy initiative. It will work far better if it is tied directly to universal coverage.

What that means in practical terms is that any plan or program put in place to achieve universal coverage for America should have embedded in it very clear requirements that having the right care-related data for each patient be included as a goal and tool of the overall health delivery improvement agenda. Simply setting up a bunch of new, isolated and unconnected data silos as we cover additional people would be a major loss of opportunity and a significant loss of care improvement leverage. We need very high standards of data security and medical privacy — and we need to be sure that data is used to support and improve care — and we need tools that make care support data available for the patients and the caregivers.

DATA SHOULD BE LONGITUDINAL

Data in the new world of functional care reform should be longitudinal. Data should follow the patient and not be automatically truncated every time a patient changes health plans or health care providers.

To be longitudinal, the data needs to be designed to be transferable. That work is entirely possible. Banks and other financial institutions have solved key issues of transportability and interoperability long ago. This isn't a new idea. It is a new approach for health care, however. Some transportability requirements will need to be established.

It won't be as hard as some people think. All health plans and payers — including Medicare, Medicaid, and SCHIP, who participate in the new universal coverage reform focused environment — should be required to produce a standard set of Personal Health Records (PHRs) for each member, beneficiary, and patient, and those PHRs should be set up so that they can be transferred easily from system to system when patients change carriers, plans, or programs.

Let's not move to universal coverage without requiring all parties who participate in the new world of universal coverage to also be part of an agenda of universal accountability, universal data flow, and macro, system-wide, care improvements.

To achieve those goals, we need a restructured, fully competitive market-place that has an interoperable and interconnected database between health plans, health insurers, care teams, and various providers of care.

WHAT KINDS OF HEALTH PLANS SHOULD COMPETE?

If America does choose to use a European universal coverage model of having health plans of one kind or another compete with each other for patients and members, we should also ask ourselves the question: "What kind of health plans and care teams should be competing in America?"

The answer to that question is a lot more obvious today than it was a decade ago. Ten years ago, we really did not appreciate how inconsistent, undependable, unaccountable, and disorganized care was in America. Today we know that those problems exist, so we know that we need a whole new level of competition in health care. Since the goal of the competition should be improving the actual quality and efficiency of care delivery, we also can now conclude that the optimal set of competitors in our new health care marketplace should be actual high performance care systems that are competing with one another at the patient level. We need caregiver teams who improve care. A new market environment that allows care delivery systems to become functional health plans — accepting premiums and providing transparent and integrated packages of care — has its own obvious value. If the best caregivers in each community can organize as a care team and then serve patients as a prepaid, financially incented care team, patients will benefit and care will get better.

So any market model for American health care or health insurance that creates real barriers to entry for provider-based care teams should be avoided. And a market model that facilitates entry by legitimate care teams should be encouraged. There should be room in that market model for both competing care teams and for a next generation of value-enhanced health plan/health insurers.

This book has pointed out that most caregivers in America do not function naturally as teams. For those caregivers we need a connection tool. Someone needs to be accountable to make sure that valid connection tools exist and are used. A next generation of health plans can and should act as market facilitators to provide consumer access to the solo practice care providers — using tools (like care registries) that link the caregivers as needed for patients who need linked care. The plans that play that "health plan" role can take financial risk and perform the needed functions relative to structuring informed choices for consumers, producing personal health records from their claims payment database, and performing all of the operationally necessary administrative duties relative to membership records, actuarial data, etc. The next generation of health plans and health insurers should compete based on their ability to support the organization of key elements of care and on their ability to make care choices transparent for consumers.

NO ONE IS ACCOUNTABLE IF NO ONE IS ACCOUNTABLE

A new generation of health insurers could play a significant role in a well-structured marketplace.

We know this to be true: Someone needs to be accountable for the cost and quality of care or no one will be accountable for the cost and quality of care. Well-structured vertically integrated care systems can take on that role easily and directly. But where there are no functioning accountable care systems, a new generation of health plans needs to take on that role. Health plans — functioning as insurers — can accept risk, spread risk, manage and facilitate care coordination, manage and facilitate data flow to consumers, and basically add value relative to disease prevention, patient education, and administration of services.

The caregivers on each team within the health plan network should be connected — with their patients and with their team facilitator.

All the connections between the new health plans and caregivers should be electronic — cutting American health care administrative costs hugely and facilitating the easy flow of care and data about care.

Care systems functioning as accountable care teams can and should play a major role in the next generation of health coverage choices. Care systems can take risk, assume accountability, deliver care, and re-engineer care — all with the patient as the focus of their care design and agenda.

"INSURANCE EXCHANGES" SHOULD OFFER CARE TEAM OPTIONS

For consumers, a market access "insurance exchange" model that allows each consumer to have real choices — and to have real and solid data about each of those choices — would be a major improvement over the market model we have today. Being able to choose as a consumer and a patient between real, functional, vertically integrated health teams and virtually integrated health teams will create a market environment that causes, incents, and rewards both vertically and virtually integrated teams as they get continuously better on both price and performance.

"Package" purchases of care make more sense financially, structurally, economically, and operationally than selling care entirely by the procedure or piece.

Having either a health plan or care team paid the equivalent of a performance premium to incent both efficiency competition and price competition is a very good idea. Premium competition is easy to administer in the context of an "insurance exchange" because premium is easy to understand and easy to collect. It's also easy to distribute.

Fee for service pay approaches can make sense for some aspects of care inside each care network, but the basic overall payment approach from the buyer needs to create a market for packages of care rather than pieces of care. Prepayment — or "premiums" — are the best payment model for incenting team care. Risk adjusted prepayment approaches are even better because well-designed risk adjuster formulas pay more for sicker patients and encourage the best provider teams to enroll the highest need patients. The competing health plan model used in The Netherlands has a risk adjustment factor built in, so the Dutch health plans that do the best job on care and enroll the sickest people are not forced into bankruptcy by their risk pool.

Within the new American health plans, payment to network providers should be structured to facilitate both connectivity and a focus on desired outcomes. Creativity in both structure and cash flow will abound when the goals of reducing kidney failure, blindness, heart crises, and asthma attacks are transparent and clear and when risk adjusted premium-like payments are made to care teams to deliver that care.

Chapter 5 listed the virtues of the Perfect IT System. As we go forward to reform health care in America, we also should decide to build the "The Perfect Competitive Care Market," with care team choices embedded in a market model that facilitates choice and enables true value-based competition.

Care will get better if we use that kind of market model for our care choices. Each of those "exchange" markets should be set up at the local level, to encourage local competition between teams of local caregivers. National purchasers should be able to use "selection facilitators" that generate computerized access to local markets, or national purchasers should be able to choose well-managed national insurance administration partners who create their own mechanisms to facilitate both choice and well-connected care.

Each community should have its own "coverage connector" or "exchange" that will allow consumers to make informed choices between competing health plans and competing care teams.

If we try to reform care by simply covering everyone in America but leave our current market model in place for care, we will be making a mistake. We need competition between care teams and caregivers based on quality, outcomes, process, and price. We also need our insurers to compete on care improvement successes rather than simply echo each other based on pure and transactional insurance structures or processes. In just about every industry, well-structured competition improves both products and prices. We need both price and product improvement in health care, so we need to structure that marketplace very carefully and very well.

In any case, coverage and care improvement in America should be a package, not two separate programs, and consumers should have informed choices of caregivers and care teams as part of that package.

The well-structured "exchange" will be another key tool to make reform happen.

7

Risk Sharing Works
Quite Well, Thank You

In roughly 30 small villages in Uganda, there are tiny, little, very local health plans. The plans are cooperatives, started by the local people for the local people and owned collectively by the local people in each village who join them.[1]

Each cooperative runs itself. Each has a governing board. Each functions as a local purchasing pool — using the collective purchasing power of the co-op members to get a good package price for care delivery from the local doctor or hospital.

Uganda does not have an extensive health care infrastructure.

Some of the hospitals who work with the co-ops have no hot water and electricity that comes from a generator on the hospital grounds. The care sites tend to be very small and fairly basic. Patients bring their own bedding most of the time.

But those hospitals are a lot better than no care at all for the local villagers. The local caregivers who run those hospitals tend to very much like the idea of local villagers banding together to collectively buy care, because there is no other health insurance in those areas of Uganda and most people are extremely poor. Bad debt is a huge problem for Ugandan doctors and hospitals.

The local caregivers — usually a tiny hospital and at least one physician — sell care to the co-ops as a package — not piece by piece and fee by fee.

RISK POOLING IS THE KEY

It's a very clear system. It's essentially a "capitation" plan. It is a "pooling" approach to care financing. It works and survives because it pools the purchasing power of the co-op members and it pools the medical risk levels for a defined population of patients in each village.

"Pooling" the risk is essential to the survival of each co-op. In order for the microhealth plans to survive, each must create a risk pool that contains both sick members and healthy members, so that the average cost of care in each village is affordable.

They need a local risk pool of premium-paying covered people that includes people who are healthy as well as sick. If only the people who are pregnant — or the people with active AIDS — enrolled in each co-op, the prepaid amount of roughly one dollar per person per month for premium payments would be totally inadequate.

The care providers and the Ugandan villagers all understand very clearly that risk pools don't work when everyone in the risk pool is sick. The villagers know very well that to keep their co-op premium levels down, each co-op needs to collect enough dollars in monthly premiums from healthy people who aren't receiving care so that there is enough total money to pay for the people who do need care.

CO-OPS SET QUOTAS

That means that the co-op starting up in each village doesn't initially kick off and become operational as a health plan until enough people have enrolled to create a viable risk pool. The minimum number set in each village is usually an enrollment of 75 percent of the relevant population.

That fact, all by itself, creates quite a bit of energy and activity on the part of the lead families who are organizing each local plan because those families very much want health coverage for their kids for the first time in their lives. The organizing families in each Ugandan village tend to work hard to get 75 percent of their friends and neighbors to enroll in the co-op and then they work hard to help people stay enrolled. It's a cooperative effort in every sense of that term.

The goal of each village co-op is to use everyone's premium payment collectively to help whoever needs help at any given point in time.

Each of the co-ops knows that as the cost of caring for all of the co-op members goes up, the premium levels also must go up to match the expenses. A "bad" risk pool in any village will simply kill the plan in that village. And people will have no insurance at all.

UGANDANS UNDERSTAND THE COST/ PREMIUM CONNECTION

Many Americans do not recognize the fact that health care cost increases are what cause health care premium increases. The Ugandan villagers know every person in their risk pool and they see that relationship very clearly. Each co-op takes careful and logical steps to both create and protect their own risk pool.

People who see the direct relationship between care costs and monthly premium — and people who pay the entire monthly premium themselves from a very meager personal cash flow — tend to make wise decisions about their own health and about the specific costs faced by their local risk pool.

Risk pools in Uganda are a wonderful tool, treasured and protected by the people who would not have coverage without them.

BLAME YOUR FEVER ON YOUR THERMOMETER

We are a bit more insulated in the United States from the immediacy of those relationships, but the same principles apply here. Health insurance premium inflation in America is almost entirely and completely the result of health care cost inflation. When health care costs go up, premiums go up. Care costs drive premiums — in the United States and in Uganda. Some people in America get the two factors confused and blame increasing health care costs on increasing health care premiums. That is exactly backward. Blaming premiums for health care costs is a little like blaming your fever on your thermometer. There is a linkage, but it's exactly the opposite of the one some people believe exists.

THE BASIC BUSINESS MODEL OF INSURANCE

So why is any of that information about Ugandan risk pool relevant to health care costs in America? Some people believe that the basic business model of private health insurance everywhere is inherently built on the principal of "risk avoidance." Risk avoidance is frequently described as being an essential part of any health insurance business model.

We've all heard that statement made: "The basic business model of American health insurance is to avoid risk." Is that true? And is risk avoidance an inherent consequence of any use of a private-insurance-based health care financing model in any marketplace?

THE KEY IS SPREADING/SHARING RISK

No. It is not true. Risk avoidance does not have to be a key component of private health insurance. The Uganda co-op model isn't based on risk avoidance. It's based on spreading risks. Sharing risk. Not "avoiding" risk. Quite a few other industrialized countries have proven that a private health insurance risk pooling model can be used to work perfectly well to create universal coverage. Those countries use private health insurance plans to cover their entire population and each of the countries uses those health plans with absolutely no health screening or risk avoidance techniques of any kind.

The key is spreading risk — sharing risk — not avoiding risk. The proof of that particular statement is all around us. Most countries in Europe currently use private competing health plans to achieve universal coverage. In Germany, every citizen is required by law to enroll in a private, non-governmental health plan. Those plans are charmingly called "Sickness Funds." Chancellor Bismarck invented them (and named them) over a century ago. They still work.

Likewise, in the Netherlands, every single citizen must enroll in a private Dutch health plan — a private insurance company.

In each of the countries where everyone is required by law to purchase private health coverage, the poor people — people with low to moderate income levels — have their coverage subsidized. Otherwise they would be required to buy something they could not afford to buy. That's obviously a bad approach.

Some countries in Europe have completely eliminated all government-based health coverage and use only private insurers. The Netherlands used to have a mixed model with both private insurers and a government program for poor people that looked a lot like Medicaid in the United States. The Netherlands government-run model didn't work very well, so the Dutch eliminated the government portion of their health plan and they now simply require everyone — rich or poor — to buy private insurance. They very wisely subsidize the cost of premiums for low-income people.

In Switzerland, they use that same completely private insurance plan model to cover all citizens. The basic rule is that all Swiss must join a private health plan — and low-income people in Switzerland get their premium subsidized so they can afford to join a plan.

The Swiss have over 70 competing health plans in that relatively small country. The plans compete aggressively for patients and members. Ads on Swiss TV for health plans look a lot like ads on U.S. TV for health plans. Competition is fierce.

SWISS REJECTED CANADIAN MODEL

The Swiss held a national referendum on their health plan agenda and approach a couple years ago. Some Swiss citizens wanted the country to convert from their current market model of multiple private competing health plans to adopt instead the Canadian model of health care. Canada, of course, uses just a single payer and has no health insurers.

The proposal to change from private insurance to a clone or echo of the Canadian single payer model lost by a 71 percent vote of rejection.[2] The Swiss were apparently happy to cover everyone using both private insurance plans and premium subsidies for low-income people.

So that raises an obvious question. How can so many European countries cover everyone in the country using private health plans as their basic financing mechanism, with no risk screening at all — while we in America don't cover nearly 50 million people and we tend to think that private health plans in America need to reject sick people for coverage as a core element of their basic business model?

THE DOUBLE MANDATE

The answer is the *Double Mandate*. Those European countries all use a double mandate — *Mandate One*: Everyone MUST buy coverage; *Mandate Two*: Every private plan MUST sell coverage to anyone who applies. Two mandates: Everyone must buy. Everyone must sell. It takes both mandates to make that model work. When both are in place, the whole process works well.

Very much like Uganda where each local co-op couldn't be activated as a health plan until the local risk pool was 75 percent enrolled, the European countries simply and clearly require everyone to be in the risk pool. When that happens, every private insurer has a wide range of sick and healthy members to spread the risk across, so everyone in each country can be enrolled in a private plan regardless of health status.

WHY DO AMERICAN INSURERS SCREEN RISK?

So why do American insurers use risk screening techniques in enrolling members here? The unfortunate truth is that we don't have a double mandate here. That's one major problem. America has absolute zero when it comes to citizen or health carrier mandates. America does not mandate that everyone — or anyone — buy coverage. So some people in America choose to be uninsured. That's where the problem starts for American risk pools.

Keep in mind that health care costs are not evenly distributed — in the United States or anywhere else in the world. In the United States, roughly 1 percent of our population runs up over 30 percent of our costs.[3] About 5 percent run up about 50 percent of our costs[4] and 10 percent of our people

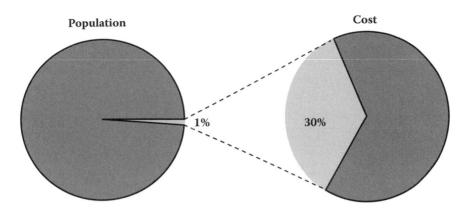

Population　　　　　　　　　　　　　　　　**Cost**

1%　　　　30%

**$300 per month average cost to cover everyone
(Break-even cost of insuring just one percent: $9,000 per month)**

Figure 7.1　Cost Distribution of Care

run up about 80 percent of our costs.[5] Those numbers create a stark reality about risk selection.

Let's look at some important numbers. A couple of years ago, based on a specific benefit package, it was calculated that if the entire population of California — except for the seniors on Medicare — was enrolled in health care coverage, the average premium cost needed to cover every single person in the state would be $300 per person.[6] That was the "break even" cost of covering everyone.

So, in other words, a health plan that covered every single Californian under 65 years old could charge $300 per month per person in premium and the plan would break even financially.

However, the problem was that if only a subset of the population enrolled, the average cost level per enrolled person could change dramatically, simply based on the costs incurred by the people who actually enrolled in the plan. The new premium need for the health plan would have to be based on the average cost of the people who actually enrolled. Remember, 1 percent of the total population used about 30 percent of the total care dollars in California that year. (See Figure 7.1.)

What would happen to average costs of care for the enrolled people if that most expensive one percent were the only people who enrolled in the health plan? The new premium that would be needed each month (to simply break even) to cover just that most expensive one percent of the risk pool would be $9,000 per person per month. Why? Because those folks are 30 times more expensive than the average cost for the rest of the people of California. That's $9,000 each month in care costs for each and every one of those members who actually joined the risk pool.

Annualized, that would require a premium of $108,000 per year per person for the health plan that enrolled those people just to break even on the cost of care for that one percent. That's a lot of money. Obviously, very few people would or could choose to pay more than $100,000 a year for their own health coverage premium, so the subsequent voluntary enrollment in that plan would probably not be very high. That would, in fact, probably be a very hard plan to sell in the voluntary marketplace. A plan that enrolled people but charged each enrollee only the original $300 per month premium would, of course, lose $8,700 per month for each and every member they enrolled. That plan obviously would not survive economically — unless the government allowed it to print money to offset cost deficits. That is not likely to happen.

Having only one percent of the population enroll is an extreme example. But similar numbers happen to the needed break-even premium level if only the most expensive 10 percent of the population were to enroll. Again, look at the numbers. The most expensive 10 percent of our population make up about 80 percent of our costs, so the new premium for those people would need to be about eight times higher than the average premium cost we could charge if we were covering everyone. That very high premium would not be a "profitable" premium. That's an eight times higher premium for the new risk pool simply to allow the health plan who enrolled those people to break even on the costs of care needed by those specific enrollees. Ten percent of Californians is a lot of people when you count heads. It would also be a massive expense load if only the top 10 percent enrolled in the plan.

LARGE NUMBERS ARE NOT MAGIC

Some people believe that bringing together large numbers of enrollees will always magically reduce average costs. That is very provably wrong. Ten percent of the people of California is a very big number, but the costs of

DILBERT: © Scott Adams/Dist. by United Feature Syndicate, Inc.

Figure 7.2   Dilbert Cartoon

care would still be eight times higher — not eight times lower or even a penny lower — if the most expensive 10 percent of the California population were the only enrollees who joined the health plan.

That concept of high care costs creating high premiums for plans enrolling sick people just seems wrong to some people. Some people who do magical thinking about health care premiums believe very strongly that there is some absolute, unexplainable miracle of numbers and dollars that simply happens and gets invoked and activated by some undefined and highly mysterious force just by "pooling" enough of anything. Some people say with great conviction in public settings that whenever the number of covered lives grows, the average cost per covered life should go down (see Figure 7.2).

RISK POOLS DON'T CURE CANCER

Unfortunately, that is not true. It is, in fact, very obviously not true. It's a little bit like house loans. Lumping a lot of bad loans into one big loan fund doesn't make any of those bad loans better. Likewise, if you take a pool of 10,000 cancer patients, there is nothing magical about the total cost of insuring those 10,000 patients that will happen just by someone putting them all in a risk pool together. Risk pooling does not fix bad loans and it does not cure cancer. It also doesn't reduce the risk of cancer. Or the individual patient cost of treating cancer. Risk pooling, in fact, doesn't impact cancer at all. So putting large numbers of cancer patients in a risk pool doesn't change the total cost of care for that risk pool at all. Large numbers do not magically reduce costs.

POOLING SMALL GROUPS ISN'T MAGIC, EITHER

Likewise, taking a large number of very high-cost small employers who have a lot of older or less healthy employees and simply lumping them together into a new larger small group risk pool doesn't somehow create a magical new lower average cost of care for small groups. Quite a few people have said that they believe that "pooling" high-cost small groups will somehow magically reduce the average care costs for each group. Not true. Pooling has no medicinal value. When pooling actually does work to lower costs, it's because the pooling process has actually added some additional number of lower cost people — new patients without cancer — to the risk pool, not because insurance pooling cures cancer. Pooling worked in Uganda because the risk pool added healthy people — not because the risk pool enrolled a large number of sick people.

Having said that, pooling does work for insurance plans in several European countries. Why? Because the risk pool there includes everyone — all the people with cancer and all the people without cancer. Everyone in the country is in those European risk pools and so the double mandate in those countries works.

So why isn't that same market dynamic and actuarial reality true of American health insurance today?

95 PERCENT DEFINES THE BUSINESS MODEL

This particular point surprises most people: European model risk sharing actually is already true, in place, operational, and fully functional in this country far more often than most people think. Right now, in fact, pure risk pooling with no health screening is currently the preferred business model for most private health insurance in America. Risk-screen-free enrollment is already true for well over 90 percent of the people who are privately insured in this country.

That is definitely not what most people believe — but look at the actual numbers. Who has health insurance in America and how did they get their insurance? Look at Figure 7.3.

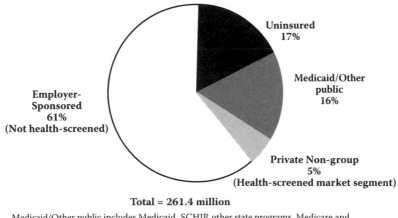

Total = 261.4 million

Medicaid/Other public includes Medicaid, SCHIP, other state programs, Medicare and military-related coverage. Data may not total 100% due to rounding.

Figure 7.3   Health Insurance Coverage of the Nonelderly Population, 2007

Most current American private health plan enrollees never went through any level of risk screening. Only the five percent who now have individual coverage were risk screened. The numbers are clear. Well over 90 percent of privately insured Americans have already acquired their current coverage with no health screen. Why is that true? Because most Americans with private coverage enroll now as members of groups.[7] That's how group coverage works. Everyone is covered. Just like in Europe. When insurers enroll an employee group in America, the insurers simply cover everyone who enrolls from the group. So it is obviously and provably true that the business model of covering basically everyone in a group works just fine as an economic approach for American health insurers just like it works for European health insurers. Screening isn't used or needed when everyone is in the risk pool. Most Americans now get health coverage through groups — and health screening doesn't need to happen when everyone in the group enrolls. Look at Figure 7.3 for proof of that statement.

FIVE PERCENT OF PRIVATELY INSURED PEOPLE HAD HEALTH SCREENS

Risk screening does happen in America. We all know that to be true. What people forget is that the health insurance risk screening done today in America applies only to the portion of the American people who buy individual coverage — not group coverage. Why would that be true? In America, individuals have no personal mandate to be covered, so all people who buy individual coverage here buy that coverage voluntarily. That means that there can be a very real potential in the individual sales part of the insurance market that people will not feel a need to buy coverage until they are already sick and need care. If they are already sick and apply for individual coverage, odds are good that they will get rejected as a purchaser of that coverage.

Having quite a few people who are sick apply for coverage and then get rejected in the individual insurance market creates a lot of very understandable public policy tension about the role and status of private health insurance in America.

Risk screening is a very immediate and personal issue for the 20 percent of the individual coverage applicants who seek to buy coverage and are now rejected for that coverage based on their own personal health status.[8]

It's a relatively small percentage but it is way too many people. We need reform very quickly to get everyone in America in the risk pool so we can make future risk screening for the 20 percent of the 5 percent of all patients irrelevant and unnecessary. We need to make that screening go away.

How would health plans in America feel about that development? Most health plans and health insurers would welcome moving that final 5 percent of the market to the same business model they already use for 95 percent of the people they already cover with no health screens. The preferred model for most health plans is actually to be inclusive, not selective, in issuing coverage.

Very few people in American health policy circles currently believe that statement to be true. But look at how the business model for health insurance actually functions. For the vast majority of covered Americans, there is now no health screening for their coverage. It's against the law, in fact, to health screen employees or to reject people with employer-based coverage for health conditions. Groups have special status. Everyone in the group is in — cancer or no cancer.

The percentage of insurance coverage chart is interesting to study. Medicare has no health screen, so everyone eligible is enrolled. Medicaid actually has an enrollment bias in favor of sick people. Poor people who are sick are sought out by Medicaid and have special eligibility. And for private insurance, all of the people with group coverage have no health screen.

That model of enrolling everyone in a group and that requirement to cover everyone in the group works just fine for insurers in America because each of those risk pools already has its own built-in version of the European double mandate — everyone in those employer groups must enroll and each health insurer who covers them must take everyone. (Some insurers allow groups to form with less than 100 percent enrollment of the employees from a given employer, but in those less-than-complete employee groups there is usually a required fixed quota of roughly 90 percent enrollment or the entire group is disbanded.)

HASSLES AND DISAGREEMENTS ARE MINIMIZED WITH INCLUSION

Enrolling everyone in a group is a clear and simple system. Insurers love it. Everyone is in. Enrollment is easy. There are no hassles or disagreements about health conditions or prior health histories. There's no risk evaluation administrative burdens or expense loads. It's simpler, easier, and it works really well as an actuarially valid business model for insurers.

So why are some applicants for insurance coverage in American health care still screened, and why do so many people believe the overarching business model for health insurers in this country is based on risk avoidance? It's an issue of risk pool protection and affordability of premium in today's individual market.

INDIVIDUAL ENROLLEES HAVE INDIVIDUAL MOTIVATIONS

Remember, the people who do not have group coverage in America are usually buying their individual coverage on a purely voluntary basis. Voluntary means that not everyone is buying that coverage. Some people can't afford to buy individual coverage — and they choose not to. Price is very important when people have to spend their own after-tax money to buy their health insurance.

People who do choose to buy personal coverage have various personal motivations and personal circumstances. People who decide to buy individual health coverage with their own money may just want the peace of mind that comes from having coverage — or they could also be people who are already pregnant or who already have cancer or who already have learned that they need a heart transplant, and they — very understandably — now recognize very clearly the upcoming costs to their own checkbook of being uninsured. At that point, they want to use someone else's money to pay for their care.

USING SOMEONE ELSE'S MONEY IS OFTEN ATTRACTIVE

Using someone else's money to pay for your care is a very human thing to do. Anyone who discovers they have congestive heart failure would much rather have the care they need paid for by someone else. So uninsured people with those kinds of expensive health issues often want to buy or get coverage from someone. The personal bank account math is pretty simple. Instead of using their own money to pay for a $100,000 triple by-pass surgery, they want to pay $500 or $1,000 in monthly premium fees and then use someone else's money to pay for the actual surgery. Care in America is expensive and direct payment for major health problems can have a huge cost. So people who have real expenses and no health insurance naturally would very often like to have someone else pay for their care at that point in their lives.

EXPENSIVE NEW MEMBERS INCREASE AVERAGE COSTS

If a bunch of new sick people simply wait until they are sick and then decide to join an existing insurance risk pool, the costs of care needed to pay the higher care expenses for the brand new enrollees will immediately raise the average cost of care for the entire existing risk pool. Premiums are always based on the average cost of care. Any increase in the average costs of care in a risk pool makes the premiums go up for everyone else who is in that particular pool.

DEATH SPIRALS CAN BE UNFORTUNATE

So that's basically why U.S. health insurers generally use health screens for their individual sales products — to keep premiums low and affordable for the people who are already in those individual market risk pools. It's not at all altruistic. It reflects business reality for the insurers. If premiums for any single risk pool go up too much, many people in that risk pool will simply cancel their coverage. Insurers then not only lose money, they lose customers.

Most alarmingly, the people who move away first when premiums go up are usually the lowest-cost people in the risk pool. Again, that makes perfect sense. The healthiest people cancel coverage first exactly because they are healthy.[9] They have no current health care costs, and they do not want to pay the higher premiums that are created when sicker people join their risk pool.

If all the really healthy people in a risk pool decide the new premium is too high and leave the risk pool, the average cost for the remaining people in the risk pool is even higher — so more leave.

That set of decisions and behaviors creates what is commonly referred to as an "actuarial death spiral." Remember how high the premiums would need to be if only the most expensive one percent of the population were in the risk pool.

An actuarial death spiral destroys a risk pool, drives healthy people away from the pool, causes fewer people to be insured, and makes premium costs painfully high for any people remaining in the pool.

Insurers in America generally try to prevent that risk pool death spiral from happening in their own piece of the individual coverage market by trying to protect their risk pools. To do that, they generally use "health screens" when new people apply to enroll in each nongroup risk pool. They use the health screens to make sure that the cost of the new people being added to the pool doesn't significantly increase the average cost of care and premium for people already in the risk pool.

That kind of risk pool selection and protection dilemma is not an issue for employer groups in America, because everyone in the group enrolls, and because everyone in the group generally stays enrolled in the group if group premiums go up. No death spiral — no health screen.

A SINGLE MANDATE CAN DESTROY RISK POOLS

How do we fix the problem of health screening in America? We need a Swiss-like double mandate in America. We need everyone to enroll, so risk selection problems become moot.

Simply allowing anyone to enroll without a double mandate doesn't solve the problem. It creates risk spirals. On average, the monthly premium costs in the risk pools in those states where any person can join regardless of health conditions run 57 to 264 percent higher than the premiums of comparable risk pools in states where the insurers use some kind of risk screen.[10]

THE BEST APPROACH IS TO COVER EVERYONE

We need to get rid of health screens in America. The best model for this country to use if we want to achieve that goal of eliminating health screens is probably something very much like the one they use in The Netherlands, Austria, or Switzerland — a double mandate — with everyone in each country required to buy coverage, and every health plan in each country required to sell coverage to any applicant who applies.

PEOPLE WHO NEED HEART TRANSPLANTS SHOULD GET HEART TRANSPLANTS

We need people who need heart transplants or even heart stents to have health coverage. No one in America should lose their home because of a health care bill. We need a safety net for care costs and we need everyone in the net.

Trying to build a net that doesn't have everyone in it would be a mistake. The village elders in Uganda understand that the risk pool has to be inclusive in order to work. Let's be ultimately inclusive here, too.

8

Focus, Tools, and Better Health

We can't fix everything in health care at once. In a perfect world, patients with stage three lung cancer would be able to choose between oncologists and treatment options based on the historic track record of each care delivery choice on both their own anticipated life span and on the likely quality of life that would result from each treatment option.

Those kinds of choices are possible. There are clear differences in survival rates for various cancer treatment programs and options. But consumers today don't have a clue about the probable outcomes or the relative success levels of the various choices they face. Or don't face.

Care programs can differ significantly in outcomes. For cystic fibrosis, a debilitating disease that shortens life spans considerably, the difference in years of survival between the least successful programs and the most successful programs is huge — ranging from slightly over 30 years of survival at the bottom of the scale to more than 40 years of survival at the top of the scale.[1] (See Figure 8.1.)

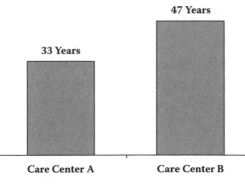

Figure 8.1   Cystic Fibrosis Life Span

Mortality rates for breast cancer surgery patients can vary by up to 60 percent depending on which hospital does your surgery.[2] Mortality rates for coronary artery by-pass surgery can vary by over 900 percent between adjacent hospitals.[3] If you are a heart patient, your personal chance of dying from that surgery is hugely different based on the hospital and surgery team you pick.

Your chance of getting a bloodstream infection after the surgery also varies by factors of 4 to 10 between comparable hospitals in the same community.[4] Bloodstream infections probably caused 70,000 deaths in California hospitals last year[5] — and consumers don't know which hospitals do the best job of keeping those infections from happening.

Most of that relative care performance data isn't currently known to consumers who need care. Very little comparative data is even available to the caregivers. We currently do not have a database in America that we can use to track results over populations of patients or populations of communities. We don't have the data we need to consistently track the outcomes of individual hospitals and relevant physicians for most care conditions.

So we, as patients, currently do not have the marketplace we should and could have relative to either patient choices or the value of care. We don't have a marketplace for care that rewards the best caregivers for the best outcomes or penalizes the caregiver whose death rate or outcome levels are significantly worse than the community norm.

America should create that market. It is a market that could be created. If we decide to create it, that work could fairly easily be done. We could identity a dozen key pieces of data — like months of survival from lung cancer or breast cancer — and begin to collect the information about relative provider performance from our current insurance claims database.

Consumers would benefit and care would get better if we begin to collect that kind of data and then use it.

BEGIN WITH CHRONIC CARE

But that's not where we should start today to do health care reform. Those are not the biggest opportunities we face in improving care. Health care costs are becoming unaffordable for many purchasers of both care and coverage, and we need to use our limited ability as a nation to reform anything significant in health care to focus on a few areas of "low-hanging fruit" relative to the most costly areas of poor performance today. Medicare will be financially impaired if it continues on its current spend rate. As our first priority, we need to fix care in those areas where fixing care can make a huge difference in the downstream cost of care and improve patient outcomes at the same time.

There used to be an adage in health care circles that you could have affordable care or you could have good care, but you couldn't have both affordable care and good care. You had to pick one. That is incredibly wrong. It reflects the total ignorance of far too many caregivers about systematic process improvement. The best care should also be the most affordable care because the current, very expensive, unfocused, unorganized, idiosyncratic approach to care gives us a lot of great incidents and individual episodes of care delivery — but it gives us really inadequate, often dangerous, and, in the aggregate, extremely wasteful total patterns of care.

CHRONIC CARE IS THE FIRST PRIORITY

Our first priority right now should be chronic care. We can't fix everything in health care, so we need to fix chronic care first.

Our patients with chronic care needs consume more than 75 percent of the health care dollars in this country. America is not alone with that disproportionate level of spending for chronic conditions. The proportional use of resources by chronic care patients is actually fairly similar for other Western countries. Some data released this year at the World Economic Conference in Davos, Switzerland, showed that both China and India also have a clear majority of their health care costs and their deaths originating from chronic conditions.

Those countries have, of course, in total, much lower total costs of overall care, but well over half of their costs come from the same sets of chronic conditions that drive 75 percent of the care costs in America.[6] All of the European countries report very similar cost proportions for their chronic care patients.

So the costs of chronic care are a worldwide and growing problem.

THE LOW-HANGING FRUIT IS TO BITE THE BULLET

In this country, we know that 80 percent of the chronic care costs come from patients with co-morbidities — and that a majority of those costs come from a half dozen conditions.

We also know that we currently do a really lousy job in this country for many of the patients with those conditions — delivering inconsistent and incomplete care to those patients a painfully high percentage of the time. The Rand research, Wennberg data, IOM reports, and multiple other individual studies show that to be true.

Diabetes is our fastest growing disease. There are more diabetics in America than in any other country. (See Figure 8.2.) More than 32 percent of all Medicare costs come from diabetic patients, yet we get care entirely right for diabetics about 8 percent of the time. If we turned the 8 into 80, we could cut kidney failure in half.

Depression is also one of our top five chronic conditions. We also do a painfully inadequate job of taking care of our depressed patients. The National Co-Morbidity Study showed that 32 percent of American patients with a behavioral disorder received adequate treatment.[7] That's particularly sad because other good studies show that good treatment is effective for 70 to 80 percent of depressed patients.[8]

Chronic care will not fix itself. We need specific care improvement goals that people can understand and support — like cutting kidney failures,

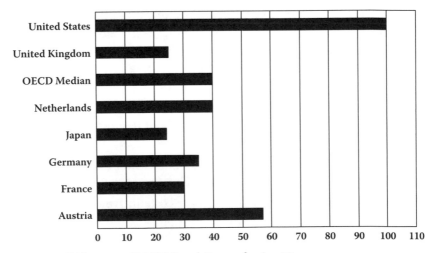

Figure 8.2   Diabetes per 100,000 Population under Age 70

heart attacks, asthma attacks, depression days from work, or congestive heart failure by half. We will need a public initiative targeted at a few key conditions, and we will need a collaborative agreement between the largest private purchasers of health coverage and the major government agencies to focus on those conditions and put the tools in place necessary to fix them. This is a time for America as a nation to step up to the challenges of becoming energy self-sufficient over time and to improve key areas of health care delivery and population health very quickly — over a matter of just a few years.

FOCUS, TOOLS, HEALTH

To achieve that goal, America needs a true public health agenda aimed at chronic care. Step 1 for the health care reform agenda in America right now should be to focus. We need to focus on the areas where we can really improve care and we should collectively set real goals to improve care outcomes in those areas.

Step 2 should be to identify and build the specific tools necessary to do that work of functional care improvement. As stated earlier in this book, tools should follow goals. Tools aren't magical. Putting tools in place without a clear sense of how they will be used or why they exist might do some good for some people some of the time, but it won't result in a systematic reform of our major cost drivers and quality problems for care.

The tools needed to improve chronic care are pretty basic. Coverage is a tool. We need everyone covered. We need coverage to incent the specific care delivery that we need to achieve our goals. Data is a key tool. We need transportable and accessible personal health record data on computers for every American. Care connectors for patients with co-morbidities are a major tool — a game-changing tool.

We need to focus on the patients who need the most support and provide those patients with the support they need. We need the patients with particular targeted diseases and co-morbidities supported by well-designed and carefully implemented care registries. Care registries can take many forms and shapes, but the key elements in each registry need to be embedded care protocols, care tracking, care-based data for each patient, and mechanisms that link caregivers for each patient with one another in a useful and meaningful way.

Some people believe that linking American caregivers is an unachievable goal. It is if we refuse to introduce any new tools to care delivery. It is entirely achievable if we change our expectation and require caregivers to coordinate care and then set up electronic tools to help that job be done.

MONEY TALKS

If we are spending $2.5 trillion on care in this country, we should expect the caregivers for each patient to be able to link up with each other in the interest of the patient.

How do we get patients and caregivers to use care registries? Money. Money and education for both caregivers and patients about the value, function, opportunity, and desirability of connectivity.

Money talks. Health care does what it is paid to do. Connectivity for certain patients should be a requirement for getting paid. Payment levels should be decreased for unconnected caregivers. Using unconnected caregivers should also trigger a benefit differentiation or a premium increase for the patients. Patients who choose to get care from unconnected providers should pay more to receive that care because unconnected providers are less likely to provide optimal care and more likely to waste the total care resources available to us all.

CHOICES SHOULD AFFECT PREMIUMS

The best way for the employee-group marketplace to have patients pay more for using unconnected providers may be in their monthly payroll deduction.

Once certain medical conditions are diagnosed and identified, patients with those conditions can be given the choice by their payer to opt to receive their care from either connected or unconnected providers, and then each patient can have his or her monthly paycheck impacted by that choice.

Over time, if patients have to pay more out of each paycheck to go to unlinked providers, the number of patients making that choice will diminish

— and that would, all by itself, be a market force that would encourage caregivers to link up.

It generally takes very few patients to move before doctors change practices to hang on to their customer base. Obviously, the tools needed to facilitate connectivity for the caregivers should be in place so that caregivers who opt for connectivity can fairly easily be connected.

Different copayments at the point of care for connected and unconnected providers can work as well. The goal of either approach is to get patients to use "connected" caregivers and to have connected caregivers working as a team to improve care.

Each payer should figure out their own approach to achieving that goal that works best for their customer base.

REGISTRIES SHOULD NOT DICTATE CARE

One essential key to the whole care improvement process is to never have either the registry or the care protocols dictate care. Care decisions should be made by each doctor and each patient working as an informed team in the full context of the doctor/patient relationship. Protocols cannot and should not practice medicine. Doctors and their patients need to decide together on treatment approaches, regardless of the counsel or direction provided by care protocols or computer support tools.

Protocols should be guidelines, not rules. Patients could well be financially penalized if they choose to get care from an unconnected provider. Patients should not be penalized if their physician and they decide to follow a course of care outside a given protocol. Illegal care would be the obvious exception to that guidance. We do not want protocols to dictate the practice of medicine.

Having patients and their physicians freely able to make individual care choices in the best interest of the patient needs to be preserved as a basic tenet of American health care, and each of the support tools used in any setting needs to function as a guidance, not a mandate.

Each decision made by patients and physicians about care approaches should be fully informed and transparent as a decision. The goal is to create consistency where consistency benefits the patient — not create consistency simply so that a protocol rule can be followed.

SCIENCE CHANGES

One of the very practical reasons for that admonition is that science changes. Medical science is constantly evolving. Drugs that were recommended one year turn out to be dangerous the next year. Hormone replacement therapy for women was a massively popular approach at one time and a therapy to be shunned a short time later. And then, after further review, that particular therapy began to find credibility for some patients some of the time. Absolute rules set for just that one area of care would have been absolutely wrong at least twice. Enforcing them as rules would have been the wrong thing to do. Guidelines relative to care delivery will never be perfect. Guidelines do, however, usually add a lot of value. We know that we can cut kidney failures by 50 percent or more if certain care guidelines are consistently followed for certain patients — so the basic value of guidelines isn't in question. But imposing specific guidelines as rigid rules for the care of each kidney patient is a very bad idea until medical science is perfect — and that day isn't here yet. It may never arrive.

In the meantime, care can get a lot better if we follow medical best practices a lot more consistently than we do now, and if we make those best practices easy to do.

9

Health May Be the Highest Priority

The first two initiatives that this book has been recommending for American health care have been (1) focus and (2) tools. Both are extremely important care improvement agendas.

The recommendation of this book up to now has been to focus on a half dozen chronic diseases, set goals for care improvement for each disease, and then put tools in place to achieve those goals.

The third key initiative that we need to focus on immediately in America is health. We need all three parts as a package to be the new care strategy for America: (1) focus, (2) tools, (3) health. Our new program for universal coverage should have focus, it should use tools, and it should be targeted at better health.

Health is, in the end, our single most important goal. Good health is everyone's basic objective. Better health needs to be the foundation and the underpinning for the entire future agenda for care. Everyone wants to be healthy. Ask people if they would choose great care or great health, and pretty much everyone would choose great health.

THE GIRTH OF AMERICA IS EXPANDING

Unfortunately, we need to do a lot better than we have been doing until now. We have a massive public health problem in America. Our chronic conditions are exploding largely because the girth of individual Americans is expanding.

The problems are basic and obvious. Obesity is a huge issue for America. Figure 9.1 and Figure 9.2 show how terrible the problem is. The number of

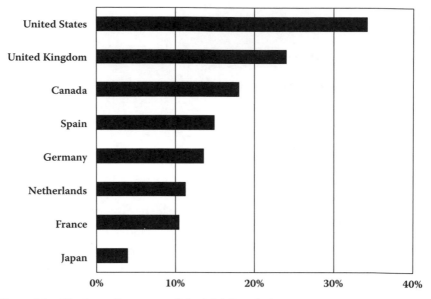

Figure 9.1   Obesity — Percentage of the Adult Population

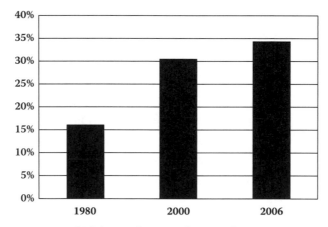

Figure 9.2   Percentage of Adults Aged 20–74 Who Are Obese

people in America who are obese (a body mass index [BMI] of 30 or above) has expanded by 40 percent in the last 10 years.[1] More than two thirds of Americans are overweight,[2] one third are medically obese,[3] and nearly 1 in 20 are morbidly obese.[4]

The statistical and medical relationship between excess weight and major health problems like diabetes, heart disease, asthma, bone problems, and several cancers is unquestioned. Fat people get sick more often.[5] America is, unfortunately, becoming fat.

The author of this book has a somewhat reinforcing personal exposure to this particular agenda — with a definite weight issue followed by quadruple heart by-pass surgery in the not-distant past. Excess weight is not good for the heart. The data shows what the data shows. The issue isn't academic and it isn't insignificant.

The opportunity is very real. If Americans weighed 20 pounds less, the number of new diabetics would shrink significantly fairly quickly.

AMERICANS ARE ALSO INERT

Activity levels are also clearly in need of reform. Americans are increasingly inert. We get very little physical activity and far too many Americans don't get the bare and basic minimal physical exercise needed to both seriously reduce heart problems and decrease the rate of becoming diabetic and suffering from various complications of diabetes.

These are not minor issues or issues we should address by simply giving talks or writing articles bemoaning obesity. Obesity and inactivity are major public health issues for America. Health care costs are exploding in large part because we are getting large.[6] Government, employers, community leaders, and individual citizens can all do something about those issues.

WE NEED A CULTURE OF HEALTH

We should address this topic as a national concern and we should create a national initiative to improve our collective health. That national agenda for health should be teed up and locked into any national agenda we set up for universal coverage. Both universal issues should be addressed, and there is real benefit in addressing them together.

We need a national culture of health. We need a president and surgeon general who take on obesity and inactivity with the same vigor that earlier health leaders in America tackled safe water, immunizations, dysentery, tobacco, and contaminated food supplies.

ELIMINATE, LABEL, REDUCE, AND PERSUADE

We need to eliminate trans fats, label and significantly reduce saturated fats, effectively and selectively tax obesity-inducing food supplies, and make sure that all segments of our population have easy access to green vegetables, and we need to encourage a cultural leaning toward eating them. We need our educational programs, schools, community centers, and large numbers of our most community-oriented religious leaders to add healthy eating to our cultural behavioral expectations.

It can be done. Creating a culture of health is possible. The people of Finland did exactly that. The Finns went from the highest rate of obesity in the Western world to one of the more reasonable levels.[7] The Finns very deliberately and strategically introduced a culture of health and made healthy behaviors a cultural expectation. It worked. Washington should lead the way, in our country. We also need the basic premises of healthy eating and higher levels of personal activity to permeate all levels of government. We very much need those agendas to be part of the value system and decision framework for every employer who buys health coverage for his or her workers. Employers should insist that their health plans work to create health, and should assign healthy behavior employee education and health improvement objectives to their human resource staff as a formal human resource goal.

This is work we all need to do. We need to incent and encourage walking. We need to incent and encourage healthy eating. There is no reason for high fat foods to be the cornerstone of the American diet for so many people. We need to literally ban trans fats, label and limit saturated fats, and make smoking so expensive that new smokers don't start and old smokers finally quit. Let economics prevail where counseling programs have failed.

We need healthy cooking, healthy food stores, and healthy items on restaurant menus. We need to work in places and settings that encourage both physical activity and good food.

All of that needs to be part of the total work done to improve health as a community. Employers can have a huge impact by building parts of that health improvement agenda into their benefit plans and work sites. Cities can build those agendas into their streets, parks, transportation systems, and open areas. Schools definitely need to go through a major rethinking of physical education, and most schools should even rethink team sports to get more people into teams. We need kids who are dancing, running, and playing ball rather than smoking, snacking, and gravitating to almost purely sedentary communal settings with minimal motion and massive physical inertia for pretty much the entire school day every single day. The damage done to students' health by the current approach is far too obvious. We need to do better. Soon.

Creative people can work on those issues. We need our leaders in all settings to recognize the value of physical activity, weight loss, and healthy eating. We need to help people take personal accountability for their own health — and to know how to make a difference in everyone's life. We need to improve our community level of health or we will not make anywhere near as much progress as we should in cutting the total costs of care in America.

WE NEED HALF AS MANY PEOPLE TO BECOME DIABETIC

We also need to set real goals for prevention. We need goals for better care outcomes, and we need equally real goals for preventing chronic disease.

This is not an ideological or philosophical position. It's an issue of extreme practicality. To keep health care affordable in America over time, we need half as many people to become diabetic — and we need to figure out exactly what we need to do in health care and in our communities to achieve that goal.

Again, the key is to start with a real goal and work backward to figure out how that goal can be achieved, rather than randomly encouraging better health and hoping that the random encouragement will somehow result in some level of health improvement for some people.

We all need to recognize the good news that it is possible to make a real difference without asking people to run marathons or lift huge weights. Walking half an hour a day, five days a week, reduces the likelihood of a person becoming diabetic by over 40 percent.[8] Walking that much and losing 15 pounds cuts the number of new diabetics by close to 60 percent.[9]

If just 40 percent fewer people became diabetic, half of the job of saving the Medicare Trust Fund would be done. Diabetics spend roughly 32 percent of the total cost of Medicare.[10] Having 40 percent fewer new diabetics could change that number significantly in a relatively short time.

WE NEED AN AGENDA OF HEALTH IMPROVEMENT

We need a culture of health. We need an agenda of health improvement. We need our employers to mandate that their health plans offer programs to improve health, and we need our schools and workplaces to encourage physical activity.

Remember, Finland has already proven that this work can be done. Finland stepped up to the plate on this exact issue over three decades ago. The Finns had some of the worst health outcomes in the world. The death rate for heart disease was 20 percent over the world average.

Because of changing diets, ending smoking, and becoming active, the Finns now have a heart disease mortality rate 20 percent under the rest of the Western world. Finland led the way. We will never save the Medicare trust fund unless we go down that same path. It can be done. (See Figure 9.3.)

Health should be our agenda — not our nemesis and our regret. We need to set some goals for community health improvement and then we need to take the steps necessary to achieve those goals. This will take national leadership. It will take linkages to our agenda of universal coverage. It is the right thing to lead. Change comes to mind.

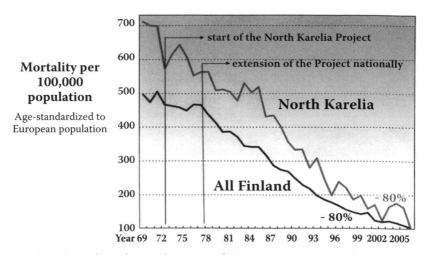

Figure 9.3   Age-Adjusted Mortality Rates of Coronary Heart Disease in North Korea and the Whole of Finland among Males Aged 35–64 Years from 1969 to 2006

10

We Also Need to Set Goals to Directly Reduce Costs

Most health care debates in America take place in a context remarkably free of data. Opinions proliferate, prejudices and anecdotes are shared with great passion, and very few of the people actually have in hand very many of the truly relevant numbers about either care delivery or care costs.

We should do a lot better than that. We need a highly informed, data-based debate about health care costs and cost drivers in America.

We definitely should take the steps necessary to create a formal, extremely well informed, highly public, data-rich, fact-based national dialogue on health care performance and health care costs. We should have that debate as a nation. Congress and the president should create an American forum for open and transparent discussion of those topics, and — as a part of the process — we should set some real goals for the entire nation to offset, influence, and constrain the growth of the total costs of American health care.

Goals are important to each major segment of health care reform. We need goals to improve care outcomes. We need goals to improve population health. And we need a very specific set of goals to reduce the rate of increase in the cost of care. Goals lead to strategies and to real-world activities and functionality. Goals point us in a direction and help us focus our thinking. The act of setting goals helps us think about what is important. The steps needed to achieve goals point us to strategies, priorities, process, and tools.

Once we set goals, we will need initiatives to improve care and we need very specific initiatives to improve health. We also need strategies to improve costs if we also bite that bullet and address that issue of care costs very directly.

National Goal: 30% Reduction in Growth Rate
Current cost growth rate is not sustainable.

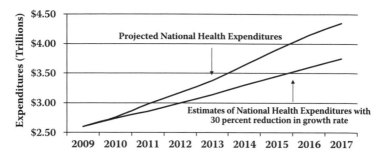

Estimated cumulative savings of more than $500B from 2010 to 2014

Reducing the rate of increase from 7 percent to 5 percent saves $1 trillion in eight years.

Figure 10.1   Reduction in Growth

So that's the other major initiative we need to establish for American health care. We need an organized public initiative to bring down the total rate of increase in the cost of care over a finite number of years.

As you can see from Figure 10.1, we don't need to actually cut the current costs of care to make a massive difference in the projected federal budget. We just need to significantly constrain the future rate of increase in the cost of care … and the long-term positive impact on the economic status of the country can be huge.

We could set a goal of actually cutting the total cost of care in America. That might be possible to do, but it is highly unlikely for all the reasons mentioned earlier in this book. But the good news is that our goal doesn't need to be to "cut" the total cost of care. We just need to reduce the rate of future growth in the cost of care. That is much more likely to happen, and the benefits of a significant reduction in the rate of increase can be huge.

If we could simply take the current projected annual rate of increase in health care costs and reduce it from 7 percent to 5 percent, that achievement alone would reduce future Medicare spending by hundreds of billions of dollars over the next few years.[1] By year 5, we would save half a trillion dollars per year for the country if we could cut the increase in the cost of care by just 30 percent — from 7 percent to 5 percent.

Figure 10.1 shows how much money we could save as a nation by just "bending the trend" and reducing the rate of increases for the total health care spending levels in America.

WE NEED A NATIONAL FORUM FOR COST REDUCTION

How can that be done? Knowledge and information are a great first step. We need to start with a fully informed public discussion of what the actual health care cost drivers in America are now, and we need an open discussion about what can really be done to bring those costs down. We need to look at every category of spending — fees, hospital costs, drug costs, imaging costs, laboratory costs, new technology costs, etc. We are ready to have that discussion and that debate.

To figure out how to "bend the trend," we need a whole new level of transparency. We need data competency. We need complete arrays of health care costs and performance data. We need to look collectively and openly at all the costs. We need, for example, to know as a nation exactly how much money is going into hospital care and what aspects of hospital expenses are projected to go up. Hospital costs are the biggest single piece of the health care spend in America.[2] We all need to know those numbers and understand what can be done to affect those numbers. If we achieve the care improvement goals outlined earlier in this book — cutting asthma crises by half, kidney failures by half, congestive heart failure crises by half, etc. — and if we reduce in-hospital bloodstream infections by way more than half, it is possible to take a lot of pressure off our hospitals and actually bring costs down for our single largest area of expense. Those very specific conversations need to be held on each of those points.

We also need to understand drug costs as a nation, looking at the total costs of prescription drugs and at the drug costs that are being projected for the future. We need to look at the potential costs of biogenetic treatments, and we need to size both their potential value and their potential cost.

Miracle treatments are possible. They may be a good idea. They will not be free. We also need to understand the cost impact of prescription drugs becoming both generic and over the counter. We definitely need to understand the projected cost increases (and the care results) that are projected from the new approaches to imaging and from various new levels of extremely high-tech surgeries and equipment.

We need to look at the full array of costs for administering health care coverage in America. America spends more money than any other country on administration of health care coverage. Those costs need to come down. Processes need to be improved. We need to figure out how to use better computer connectivity between caregivers and payers to reduce many of the directly claims-related insurance expenses — probably by 35 to 50 percent. Paper doesn't work well for medical records and it also creates a lot of administrative waste as a key part of the payment process. We need standardization and connectivity in the area of enrollments, billing, and data exchanges. Administrative costs should be lower. We all need to know those numbers and understand what we can do collectively to make those numbers smaller soon.

We need everything that creates health care costs on the table — and we need everything on the table to have a price tag attached.

Right now, quite a few health care policy debates are under way. We are also having multiple layers of discussions about specific areas of health care costs. Those specific cost debates now tend to be very "one-off" — narrow, separate, and unconnected. This book referred to the blind men and the elephant earlier. We, as Americans, now need to see the whole cost elephant. We need to put the entire health care elephant on public display under merciless spotlights with full levels of measurement and data.

How can we have that conversation and make sure that we get everything on the table?

WE NEED A COMMISSION

Congress and the president should name a National Commission on Health Care Costs whose job is to both put the whole and complete health care cost animal on public display and simultaneously identify in very specific ways what could be done to bring the total annual rate of cost increase for all health care services down to five percent — or to another equivalent number targeted by the president and Congress.

Five percent is a good number to work with. We could save half a trillion dollars a year in five years over current projections if we just brought the rate of increase for the costs of care down to an average of five percent per year. Five percent is enough money to allow needed new drugs and tests to get to the market. It's enough money to fund the data support expenses that care reform will create. It's enough money to attract workers into care giving jobs. And it is lower than current trends by quite a bit — so it puts less pressure on our economy. We would be well served by a good five percent solution.

Right now, the national and local debates about health care costs are heated but amazingly uninformed. Like the rest of health care, the discussion is largely data free. Everyone has his or her own favorite cost control data points and subpoints — and, just like the blind men and the elephant, some see a wall and others see a snake.

We all need to see the whole elephant. A well-designed and well-supported health care cost commission could do that work — and a really well-run commission could turn the splintered health care debate in America into a fully informed discussion about the actual current costs and future costs of care. The health care cost commission could give us a public setting where we could choose to do what some other Western countries have done and figure out how to make collective decisions about the cost and scope and future of our care. We need to start those discussions by really understanding what the cost realities are for care.

WE NEED COMPLETE DATA ABOUT COST DRIVERS FOR CARE

Magical thinking will not fix health care and it will not meaningfully impact health care costs. Transparent data and full understanding of the actual cost drivers could, however, help fix the major problems we face.

Until we have that fully informed national discussion, the debate about health care costs and health care coverage will continue to imperfectly inform the public, and the solutions we develop for both cost and coverage will have a tendency to also be imperfectly formed.

We also need to recognize the fact that health care can be a very good use of our money. We would not be in a bad place if we could look openly at the issue and be able to say, "Health care is getting better. Health care is a great use of our dollar — as good as clothes, cars, movies, or computer games. It creates great jobs and those jobs stabilize local economies. Let's keep a reasonable spend rate for health care and let's make very sure that care delivery is more accountable and effective."

Purchasing health is, at least theoretically, a viable and valuable use of our health care dollars. More than most other industries, health care creates good local jobs, good infrastructure, and — when done well — helps support better lives.

That conclusion might be reached by the commission. It wouldn't be the very worst outcome of the discussion to figure out how to actually get full value for our health care dollar.

THE GOAL SHOULD BE TO "BEND THE TREND"

We need to be very goal focused in this process. We need to significantly bend the cost trend for health care in America. Creative and effective solutions to fix costs will not come forward until the goal that is set makes those solutions necessary.

The commission should look at the total health care spending in America, in much more complexity, and say, "To cut the increased rate of spending for health care in America by four percent to five percent, we need to do six important things. Those six things are … and …."

Then the public and our governing bodies can look at those strategies and make informed choices about the road ahead.

HEALTH CARE COULD BE MOVING TO A GOLDEN AGE

We don't need to wait for that commission to be formed and do its work to begin improving care delivery in America. We could and should be moving quickly into very exciting times. We need to think of health care as a total agenda for positive change, and we need to convert from aimless drifting in key performance areas to focused achievement in key performance areas. We need a national health agenda that includes goals for care improvement and goals for health improvement.

Remember—The Wennberg Data, Millman Data, and the Commonwealth Research Data all showed us that we could save half a trillion dollars a year just by getting care right. We owe it to ourselves to do what needs to be done to "get care right."

If we set a national agenda to focus on chronic care, if we have the courage to put the tools in place needed to fix that care, if we work to instill a real culture of health, and then if we make the whole health care cost debate both fully informed and fully transparent with the goal of making future cost levels more affordable, America will be a better place to live and a better place to get care. We could move to a golden age of continuously improving affordable care by simply beginning to use continuous improvement methodology in the delivery and science of care.

If we computerize care record keeping appropriately, we could have a database that turns 250 million Americans into a huge, ongoing, data-rich clinical trial. We could and should become a nationwide culture of medical excellence, medical efficiency, and continuous medical improvement.

Universal coverage is needed to get us to that place. We can't get there if large portions of our population are uninsured, off the care improvement radar screen, and have inappropriate and inconsistent access to care. We need to simultaneously cover everyone, and we need to put programs in place to significantly improve care for everyone in America. Care improvement and universal coverage should be a package. The universal coverage package enacted by Congress should be anchored on a few key areas of care improvement. We need to think systematically about health and we need to improve both health and health care delivery in this country.

It can be done. It should be done. Let's do it.

Be well.

Endnotes

INTRODUCTION

1. Obama '08. "Barack Obama's Plan for a Healthy America: Lowering Health Costs and Ensuring Affordable, High-Quality Health Care for All." http://www.barackobama.com.
2. The Kaiser Family Foundation and Health Research and Educational Trust, "Employer Health Benefits, 2007 Summary of Findings." September 2007. http://www.kff.org/insurance/7672/index.cfm, Exhibit B: Average Annual Firm and Worker Premium Contributions and Total Premiums for Covered Workers for Single and Family Coverage, by Plan Type, 2007.
3. L. Nichols and P. Harbage. "Estimating the 'Hidden Tax' on Insured Californians due to the Care Needed and Received by the Uninsured." New America Foundation. May 2007.
4. A Dobson, J. DaVanzo, and N. Sen. "The Cost-Shift Payment 'Hydraulic': Foundation, History, and Implications." Health Affairs, 2006, Vol. 25, 1:22–33.
5. U.S. Bureau of Labor Statistics. "Producer Price Index Industry Data, General Medical and Surgical Hospitals, 1992–2009."
6. Centers for Disease Control. "Chronic Disease Control." http://www.cdc.gov/nccdphp/overview.htm. February 2009.
7. S. Carpenter. "Treating an Illness Is One Thing. What about a Patient with Many?" The New York Times. March 31, 2009.
8. Partnership for Solutions. "Chronic Conditions — Making the Case for Ongoing Care." September 2004 update, Johns Hopkins University. 2004.
9. The Commonwealth Fund, "Evidence-Informed Case Rates: Paying for Safer, More Reliable Care." Issue Brief, Commonwealth Fund pub. 1146, Vol. 40, June 2008, p. 6.
10. B. Pyenson and others. "Imaging 16% to 12%, A Vision for Cost Efficiency, Improving Healthcare Quality, and Covering the Uninsured." Milliman Research Report. February 2009.
11. J. Wennberg and others. "The Care of Patients with Severe Chronic Illnesses: An Online Report on the Medicare Program by the Dartmouth Atlas Project." The Dartmouth Atlas of Health Care 2006. The Center for Evaluative Clinical Sciences, Dartmouth Medical School.
12. U.S. Census Bureau. "Income, Poverty, and Health Insurance Coverage in the United States: 2007." August 2008.

CHAPTER 1

1. S. Keehan and others. "Health Spending Projections through 2017." Health Affairs Web Exclusive, W146:21, February 2008.
2. Ibid.
3. P. Orszag. "Growth in Health Care Costs." CBO Testimony before the Committee on the Budget, U.S. Senate. January 31, 2008.
4. Centers for Medicaid and Medicare Services, "Diagnosis and Procedure Codes and Their Abbreviated Titles." http://www.cms.hhs.gov/ICD9ProviderDiagnosticCodes/06_codes.asp#TopOfPage.
5. J. Wennberg and others. "The Care of Patients with Severe Chronic Illnesses: An Online Report on the Medicare Program by the Dartmouth Atlas Project." The Dartmouth Atlas of Health Care 2006. The Center for Evaluative Clinical Sciences, Dartmouth Medical School.
6. E.A. McGlynn and others. The quality of health care delivered to adults in the United States. *New England Journal of Medicine*, 2003, 348:2635–2645.
7. R. Mangione-Smith and others. The quality of ambulatory care delivered to children in the United States. *New England Journal of Medicine*, 2007, 357:1515–1523.
8. N. Kroll and others. "Disabling Childhood Asthma." Health & Disability Issue Brief. Washington, DC: NRH Center for Health & Disability Research. April 2001.
9. Committee on Quality of Health Care in America, Institute of Medicine. *Crossing the Quality Chasm*. National Academy Press. Washington, DC. 2001.
10. H. Pham and others. Redesigning care delivery in response to a high-performance network: The Virginia Mason Medical Center. *Health Affairs*, 2007, 26(4):w532–w544 (published online 10 July 2007).

CHAPTER 2

1. W. Smith. Consider communications solution for emerging labor shortage. *Managed Healthcare Executive*. February 1, 2008.
2. M. Engel. Help Wanted: U.S. Has a Shortage of Trained Health Workers, Hospitals Scramble for Pharmacy Technicians, Lab Scientists and Other Trained Workers as Baby Boomers Age and Retire. *Los Angeles Times*. July 27, 2008.
3. American Hospital Association. "Hospitals' Workforce Challenges." AHA News. http://www.ahanews.com/ahanews_app/jsp/display.jsp?dcrpath=AHANEWS/AHANews-Article/data/AHA_News_080303_Hospitals_workforce&domain=AHANEWS. March 3, 2008.
4. OECD. *Health At a Glance 2007*. November 2007.
5. Ibid.
6. K. Hauer and others. Factors associated with medical students' career choices regarding internal medicine. *Journal of the American Medical Association*, 2008, 300(10):1154–1164.

7. "Geriatric Doctor Shortage Causes Alarm." MSNBC.com. http:www.msnbc.msn.com/id/11047513/. January 26, 2006.
8. See Note 7.
9. T. Bodenheimer. Primary care — will it survive? *New England Journal of Medicine*, August 31, 2006, 335(9):861–864.
10. Ibid.
11. Ibid.
12. R. Fujisawa and G. Lafortune. "The Remuneration of General Practitioners and Specialists in 14 OECD Countries: What Are the Factors Influencing Variations across Countries." OECD Health Working Papers No. 41. OECD, Directorate for Employment, Labour, and Social Affairs Health Committee. December 18, 2008.
13. Congressional Budget Office. "Technological Change and the Growth of Health Care Spending." http://www.cbo.gov/doc.cfm?index=8947. January 2008.
14. A. Berenson and R. Abelson. Weighing the Costs of a CT Scan's Look Inside the Heart. *New York Times*. June 29, 2008.
15. L. Hilton. Quality First. *AHIP Coverage*. November/December 2008. p. 52.
16. See Note 15.
17. America's Health Insurance Plans. "Ensuring Quality through Appropriate Use of Diagnostic Imaging." http://www.ahip.org/content/default.aspx@docid=24057. July 2008.
18. The Prescription Project. "Academic Detailing: Evidence-Based Prescribing Information." October 5, 2007.
19. OECD. "OECD Health Data 2008: Statistics and Indicators for 30 Countries." December 2008.
20. Canadian Institute for Health Information. "Medical Imaging in Canada." http://secure.cihi.ca/cihiweb/dispPage.jsp?cw_page=media_21aug2008_e, Table 1: Average Number of MRI and CT Exams per 1,000 Population, per Scanner for Selected Countries, 2006–2007 or latest available year. August 2008.
21. The McKinsey Global Institute. "Accounting for the Cost of Health Care in the United States." January 2007.
22. Ibid.
23. G. Anderson. "Chronic Conditions: Making the Case of Ongoing Care." Partnership for Solutions, John Hopkins University. November 2007.
24. Ibid.
25. Centers for Medicare and Medicaid Services. National Health Expenditures data.
26. U.S. Census Bureau. U.S. Population Projections. http://www.census.gov/population/www/projections/summarytables.html.
27. The Kidney Foundation of Canada. "Kidney Disease Prevention." http://www.kidney.ab.ca/prod/index.php?option=com_content&view=category&layout=blog&id=53&Itemid=8. Accessed February 25, 2009.
28. Centers for Disease Control. "Preventing Diabetes and Its Complications." http://www.cdc.gov/nccdphp/publications/factsheets/Prevention/pdf/diabetes.pdf. Revised August 2008.
29. Ibid.

CHAPTER 3

1. G. Halvorson. *Strong Medicine*. Random House. New York. 1993.
2. J. Wennberg and others. "The Care of Patients with Severe Chronic Illnesses: An Online Report on the Medicare Program by the Dartmouth Atlas Project." The Dartmouth Atlas of Health Care 2006. The Center for Evaluative Clinical Sciences, Dartmouth Medical School.
3. Ibid.
4. N. Scarborough. "Medical Misdiagnosis in America 2008: A Persistent Problem with a Promising Solution." HealthLeaders Media Whitepaper. http://www.healthleaders-media.com/content/206010.pdf. February 2008.
5. Ibid.
6. E. Rabinowitz. Preventable. *AHIP Coverage*. November/December 2008.
7. B.G. Druss. Comparing the national economic burden of five chronic conditions. *Health Affairs*, 2001, 20(6):233–241.
8. American Academy of Allergy Asthma & Immunology. "Diseases 101: Childhood Asthma." http://www.aaaai.org/patients/gallery/childhoodasthma.asp. Accessed March 5, 2009.
9. D. Evans and others. Educating health professionals to improve quality of care for asthma. *Paediatric Respiratory Reviews*, 2004, 5(4):304–310.
10. R. Mangione-Smith and others. The quality of ambulatory care delivered to children in the United States. *New England Journal of Medicine*, 2007, 357:1515–1523.
11. J. Kennedy and others. Unfilled prescriptions of Medicare beneficiaries: prevalence, reasons, and types of medicines prescribed. *Journal of Managed Care Pharmacy*, July/August 2008, 14(6):553–560.
12. G. Halvorson. Racial Disparities & Universal Coverage. *Oakland Tribune*. Op-Ed, September 6, 2007.
13. M. McDaniel and others. Racial disparities in childhood asthma in the United States: evidence from the National Health Interview Survey, 1997 to 2003. *Pediatrics*, May 2006, 117(5):e868–877.
14. T.A. Lieu and others. Racial/ethnic variation in asthma status and management practices among children in managed Medicaid. *Pediatrics*, May 2002, 109(5):857–865.
15. Centers for Disease Control. "Child and Adolescent Mortality by Cause: US/State, 2000–2003." April 2007. http://www.cdc.gov/nchs/health_data_for_all_ages.htm.
16. B. Richman and others. Lessons from India in organizational innovation: a tale of two heart hospitals. *Health Affairs*, September/October 2008, 27(9):1260–1270.

CHAPTER 4

1. OECD. "Health at a Glance 2007." November 2007.
2. B.G. Sandhoff and others. Collaborative cardiac care service: a multidisciplinary approach to caring for patients with coronary artery disease. *The Permanente Journal*, Summer 2008, 12(3):4–11.

3. Partnership for Quality Care. "Quality, Cost Control, Universal Healthcare: Case Studies of Innovations in Chronic Care to Improve Outcomes and Contain Healthcare Costs." 2008.
4. *Seattle Post.* September 15, 2005.
5. See Note 1.

CHAPTER 5

1. C. Rauber. Raising Kaiser's Role, Vioxx Shines Light on Health Giant's Research. *San Francisco Business Times*, October 29, 2004.
2. U.S. Bureau of the Census. National, State, and Puerto Rico Population Estimates. July 1, 2008. Kaiser Permanente News Center. "Kaiser Foundation Health Plan, Inc. and Kaiser Foundation Hospitals Report Fourth Quarter and Fiscal-Year 2008 Results." February 13, 2009.
3. Kaiser Permanente News Center. "Kaiser Foundation Health Plan, Inc. and Kaiser Foundation Hospitals Report Fourth Quarter and Fiscal-Year 2008 Results." February 13, 2009.
4. R. Dell and others. Osteoporosis disease management: the role of the orthopaedic surgeon. *Journal of Bone and Joint Surgery (American)*, 2008, 90:188–194.
5. Ibid.
6. StrategyOne. "Kaiser Permanente Health IT 2008 Tracking Survey." June 2008.

CHAPTER 6

1. Congressional Budget Office. "Technological Change and the Growth of Health Care Spending." http://www.cbo.gov/doc.cfm?index=8947. January 2008.
2. C. Schoen and others. "Insured but Not Protected: How Many Adults Are Underinsured?" Health Affairs, 10.1377/hlthaff.w5.289, June 14, 2005.

CHAPTER 7

1. G. Halvorson. Health Care Co-ops in Uganda, Effectively Launching Micro Health Groups in African Villages. The Permanente Press, Oakland, 2006.
2. "Health Reform Flops at the Ballot Box." Swiss News, World Wide. http://www.swissinfo.ch/eng/swissinfo.html?siteSect=105&sid=7609812&ty. March 11, 2007.
3. Based on internal Kaiser Permanente data.
4. Based on internal Kaiser Permanente data.
5. Based on internal Kaiser Permanente data.

6. California Legislative Analyst's Office. "Health Care Reform (Review of ABX1 1 [Nunez])." January 22, 2008.
7. "Individual Health Insurance 2006–2007: A Comprehensive Survey of Premiums, Availability, and Benefits, America's Health Insurance Plans." AHIP. http://www. ahipresearch.org. December 2007.
8. Ibid.
9. The Council for Affordable Health Insurance. What were these states thinking: the pitfalls of guaranteed issue. Issues & Answers, May 2002, No. 104.
10. AHIP, Center for Policy and Research. "Individual Health Insurance 2006–2007: A Comprehensive Survey of Premiums, Availability, and Benefits." December 2007.

CHAPTER 8

1. 1997 Cystic Fibrosis Foundation Patient Registry, as reported in A. Gawande. The Bell Curve, *The New Yorker*, December 12, 2004.
2. M. R. Chassin. Is health care ready for six sigma quality? *Millbank Quarterly*, 1998, 76(4):510.
3. California Office of Statewide Health Planning and Development. "The California Report on Coronary Artery Bypass Graft Surgery 2005 Hospital Data." December 2007. http://oshpd.ca.gov/HID/Products/Clinical_Data/CABG/05Breakdown.html.
4. H. Aly and others. Is bloodstream infection preventable among premature infants? A tale of two cities. *Pediatrics*, 2005, 115:1513–1518.
5. Q. Nguyen. "Hospital-Acquired Infections." eMedicine. http://emedicine.medscape. com/article/967022-print. Updated January 14, 2009.
6. World Economic Forum. "Managing Chronic Diseases in Emerging Countries: The Case of Diabetes in China & India." Annual Meeting 2009.
7. S. Melek. An expensive correlation: the high cost of comorbid depression on employees with chronic or serious medical conditions. *Health Perspectives*. Fall 2008: 4–5.
8. Rand Health. "The Societal Promise of Improving Health Care for Depression: Nine Years Out." 2008.

CHAPTER 9

1. Centers for Disease Control, Behavioral Risk Factor Surveillance System. "Obesity Trends among U.S. Adults between 1985 and 2006." http://www.cdc.gov/brfss/.
2. Ibid.
3. Congressional Budget Office. "Technological Change and the Growth of Health Care Spending." http://www.cbo.gov/doc.cfm?index=8947. January 2008.
4. Ibid.
5. A. Di Rado. The Skinny on Fat. *USC Health Magazine*. Winter 2004.
6. See Note 1.

7. P. Puska. The North Karelia Project: 30 years successfully preventing chronic diseases. *Diabetes Voice*, May 2008, 53: 26–28.
8. Diabetes Prevention Program Coordinating Center. Diabetes Prevention Program. 2002.
9. Ibid.
10. Centers for Medicare and Medicaid. 2005.

CHAPTER 10

1. P. Orszag. "Health Care and the Budget: Issues and Challenges for Reform." CBO Testimony before the Committee on the Budget, United States Senate. June 21, 2007.
2. Congressional Budget Office. "Technological Change and the Growth of Health Care Spending." http://www.cbo.gov/doc.cfm?index=8947. January 2008.

Index

About the Author

George Halvorson has been the chief executive officer of health plans, hospital systems, and care delivery systems in the United States for over three decades. He has also helped start health plans in Jamaica, Chile, Nigeria, Spain, and Uganda.

He is the current chair of the International Federation of Health Plans and he also served as chair of the Health Governors for the 2009 World Economic Conference in Davos, Switzerland.

Kaiser Permanente, his current employer, is the largest not-for-profit health plan and care system in America — with over eight and a half million members, 160,000 employees and roughly forty billion dollars in annual revenue.

He is the past chair of the American Association of Health Plans and has served on the Board of Directors for the American Diabetes Associations, The Alliance of Community Health Plans, and Safest in America.

He also currently chairs the Alliance for Quality — and serves on the Commonwealth Commission for a High Performing Health System.

He is a long time proponent of health care reform — regularly writing articles and books and making presentations advocating reform. Recent books include *Epidemic of Care* (Jossey-Bass, San Francisco) and *Health Care Reform Now!* (Jossey-Bass, San Francisco).

Kaiser Permanente has been a pioneer in the use of electronic medical records and computer connectivity between patients and caregivers — successfully completing a four billion dollar project to computerize the medical information for its members and patients.

He is a husband, father of five sons, and grandfather to five wonderful grandchildren. He is headquartered in Oakland, California.